MODERN MEDITERRANEAN COOKING

MODERN MEDITERRANEAN COOKING

A CULINARY COLLECTION OF FRESH FLAVORS

Elena Balashova

Reader's Digest

The Reader's Digest Association, Inc.
Pleasantville, New York/Montreal/London/Mumbai

A READER'S DIGEST BOOK

This edition published by
The Reader's Digest Association, Inc.,
by arrangement with McRae Books Srl

Copyright © 2010 McRae Books Srl

All rights reserved. Unauthorized reproduction,
in any manner, is prohibited.

Reader's Digest is a registered trademark
of The Reader's Digest Association, Inc.

Modern Mediterranean Cooking was created
and produced by
McRae Books Srl
Via Umbria, 36, Florence, Italy
Info@mcraebooks.com

FOR MCRAE BOOKS
Project Director: Anne McRae
Art Director: Marco Nardi
Photography: Brent Parker Jones
Photographic Art Direction: Neil Hargreaves
Texts: Jenny Fanshaw, Annette Forrest
Food Styling: Lee Blaycock, Neil Hargreaves
Layouts: Aurora Granata
Prepress: Filippo Delle Monache,
 Davide Gasparri

FOR READER'S DIGEST
U.S. Project Editor: Andrea Chesman
Canadian Project Editor: Pamela Chichinskas
Senior Art Director: George McKeon
Executive Editor, Trade Publishing:
 Dolores York
Associate Publisher, Trade Publishing:
 Rosanne McManus
President and Publisher, Trade Publishing:
 Harold Clarke

LIBRARY OF CONGRESS CATALOGING-IN-PUBLICATION DATA

Balashova, Elena, 1954-
 Modern Mediterranean cuisine : a culinary
collection of fresh flavors / Elena Balashova.
 p. cm.
 ISBN 978-1-60652-136-6 (U.S. edition)
 ISBN 978-1-60652-184-7 (International edition)
1. Cookery, Mediterranean. I. Title.
TX725.M35B34 2009
641.59822--dc22

2009051117

We are committed to both the quality of our
products and the service we provide to our
customers. We value your comments, so please
feel free to contact us.

The Reader's Digest Association, Inc.
Adult Trade Publishing
Reader's Digest Road
Pleasantville, NY 10570-7000

NOTE TO OUR READERS
Eating eggs or egg whites that are not
completely cooked poses the possibility of
salmonella food poisoning. The risk is greater
for pregnant women, the elderly, the very young,
and persons with impaired immune systems.
If you are concerned about salmonella, you can
use reconstituted powdered egg whites
or pasteurized eggs.

For more Reader's Digest products and
information, visit our website:
  www.rd.com (in the United States)
  www.readersdigest.ca (in Canada)
  www.rdasia.com (in Asia)

Printed in China

3 5 7 9 10 8 6 4 2 (U.S. edition)
3 5 7 9 10 8 6 4 2 (International edition)

On the cover: (Main image) paella; (top left) greek salad; (top center) panna cotta with raspberry coulis; (top right) stuffed bell peppers.
Spine: paella
Back cover: (Top left) deep-fried crab balls; (top left) lamb tagine with dates; (center left) mussels with roasted tomato sauce; (center right) spinach, feta, and artichoke salad; (bottom) crepes suzette with strawberries

The level of difficulty for each recipe is indicated on a scale from
1 (easy) to 3 (complicated).

CONTENTS

INTRODUCTION

This book is a celebration of the glorious foods of the Mediterranean, from the European lands of Italy, France, Spain, the Balkans, and Greece to North Africa, the Middle East, and Turkey. Twenty-one countries border this warm, almost landlocked sea, and they are famous for many things, from their ancient cultures, magnificent historical cities, and hilltop towns to their fabulous beaches, sophisticated nightlife, and wonderful food and wine. How many of you have ever delighted in the last rays of a summer's day in a café in southern France or Spain, an enticing plate of tapas and an aperitif before you; eaten inordinately well in a little seaside *ristorante* in Italy, your feet almost dangling in the sea? Or perhaps you have dined in the open air on freshly caught fish on the terrace of a Greek taverna, indigo sky overhead. Each of you has, I should think, at least in your minds, if not in reality. Because the Mediterranean is a destination, an ambience, a mood, clearly defined in our collective heads as sunshine, history, food, wine, health, and fun.

In this book, we have sought to recreate the ambience and mood of the Mediterranean through its food, by creating modern dishes that retain the authentic flavors of the region's traditional cuisines. And because most of us have less and less time to spend in the kitchen, we have tried to choose recipes that depend more on the quality and freshness of their ingredients and efficient techniques, rather than

hours spent over a hot stove. All the recipes in this book can be prepared easily in a home kitchen, and many of them can be made in less than 30 minutes, from start to finish.

The recipes have been organized into thematic chapters, from appetizers to desserts. We begin with a substantial selection of antipasti and tapas. For a casual gathering or buffet, you may like to prepare a selection of these and serve them together with some home-baked focaccia from the bread chapter as a meal in themselves. Alternatively, you can design a meal of several courses with the traditional rhythms of a Mediterranean repast: an appetizer, followed by a soup, rice, or pasta first course, then a fish- or meat-based second course served with a side of vegetables or a salad. You can round off the meal with dessert. There are also plenty of ideas for snacks and light meals, from soups, risottos, and salads to pasta and omelet and frittata dishes. The final chapter features 18 sensational desserts, including all-time favorites such as tiramisù, lemon sorbet, baklava, and panna cotta.

To help you plan your meals, each recipe includes preparation and cooking times. We have also graded the recipes from 1 to 3 for difficulty (1=easy to 3=complicated), with most falling into the first or second categories.

With more than 200 recipes, this book embodies the celebrated Mediterranean diet and its well-known health benefits. An American doctor working in southern Italy at the end of World War II was among the first to recognize the positive effects of the traditional Mediterranean way of eating. Although the diet only became widely popular in the 1990s, long-term medical research has proved again and again that the Mediterranean diet leads to significantly lowered death rates from heart disease and cancer while also offering substantial protection against type-2 diabetes, Parkinson's, and Alzheimer's disease. Medical studies on weight loss that compared low-carb diets to the more balanced Mediterranean diet also found that the latter led to similar levels of weight loss among men and greater weight loss among female participants.

So, what is this miracle diet that is not only enjoyable and easy but also helps us lose weight while prolonging both the quality and length of our lives? The key components of the Mediterranean diet are high consumption of fresh fruit and vegetables, beans, whole grains, and olive oil, moderate consumption of fish and dairy products (mainly as yogurt and cheese), and low consumption of red meat and eggs. The "diet" is also seen as a lifestyle, with small amounts of wine consumed with meals on a daily basis, high levels of physical activity, and a convivial social atmosphere where the bonds of family and friendship are treasured and enjoyed.

Here you will find a wealth of ideas for modern Mediterranean dishes that can be enjoyed on a daily basis. Not only will they conjure up the magic atmosphere of the Mediterranean, they will also help improve your health and happiness. Enjoy!

ANTIPASTI AND TAPAS

SALTED ALMONDS

Preheat the oven to 350°F (180°C/gas 4). • Spread the almonds out on a baking sheet. • Roast until lightly browned, about 20 minutes. • Mix the egg white and salt in a small bowl. • Add the almonds, shaking well to coat them in the egg white. Pour them out onto the baking sheet, shaking to separate the nuts. • Return to the oven for 5 minutes until the almonds have dried. • Let cool completely. • Store in an airtight container until ready to serve.

1 cup (150 g) whole almonds, shelled but with their skins

1 tablespoon egg white, lightly beaten

1/2 teaspoon coarse sea salt

Serves: 2–4
Preparation: 10 minutes
Cooking: 25 minutes
Level: 1

■ ■ ■ *Serve these almonds with before-dinner drinks, such as Campari soda or kir royale (dry champagne topped up with cassis).*

EGGPLANT ROLLS

Rolls: Brush the slices of eggplant on both sides with oil. • Heat a grill pan and grill the eggplant until softened and just browned, about 5 minutes each side. Let cool slightly. • Preheat the oven to 350°F (180°C/gas 4). • Oil a large baking dish. • Mix the tomatoes, mozzarella, and basil in a medium bowl. Season with salt and pepper. • Spoon a little of the tomato mixture onto the end of each slice of eggplant and roll up. • Arrange the rolls, seam-side down, in the prepared baking dish. • Bake until the mozzarella has melted, about 15 minutes.

Dressing: Sauté the tomato in 1 tablespoon of the oil in a small saucepan over medium heat until softened, 2–3 minutes. • Add the remaining oil, balsamic vinegar, and pine nuts. Season with salt and pepper. • Cook for 1 minute until warmed through. • Arrange the rolls in a serving dish and spoon the dressing over the top. • Garnish with the basil and serve warm.

Rolls

2   eggplants (aubergines), sliced 1/4-inch (5-mm) thick

3   tablespoons extra-virgin olive oil

3   medium tomatoes, seeded and diced

5   ounces (150 g) mozzarella cheese, diced

2   tablespoons fresh basil, torn

Salt and freshly ground black pepper

Fresh basil leaves, to serve

Dressing

1   tomato, diced

1/4 cup (60 ml) extra-virgin olive oil

1   tablespoon balsamic vinegar

2   tablespoons pine nuts, toasted

Salt and freshly ground black pepper

Serves: 4–6
Preparation: 15 minutes
Cooking: 30 minutes
Level: 2

POTATO FETA FRITTERS

Mix the mashed potato, feta, egg, scallions, dill, and lemon juice and zest in a medium bowl until well combined. Season with pepper. • Cover with plastic wrap (cling film) and chill until firm, 1–2 hours. • Using your hands, roll the mixture into balls the size of golf balls, then flatten them slightly. • Dip in the flour until well coated, shaking off the excess. • Heat the oil in a large, deep frying pan. • Fry the fritters a few at a time until lightly browned all over, 5–7 minutes. • Remove with a slotted spoon and drain on paper towels. • Garnish with the extra dill and serve hot.

■ ■ ■ *These fritters are especially good when served with tzatziki (see Tomatoes Filled with Tzatziki on page 86).*

1¹/2 cups (375 g) cooked potato, mashed

4 ounces (125 g) feta cheese, crumbled

1 large egg, lightly beaten

3 scallions (spring onions), finely chopped

3 tablespoons finely chopped fresh dill + extra, to garnish

1 tablespoon freshly squeezed lemon juice

Finely grated zest of ¹/2 lemon

Freshly ground black pepper

¹/2 cup (75 g) all-purpose (plain) flour

¹/2 cup (125 ml) extra-virgin olive oil

Serves: 4–6
Preparation: 30 minutes + 1–2 hours to chill
Cooking: 10–14 minutes
Level: 1

MARINATED SARDINES

Preheat the oven to 350°F (180°C/gas 4).
• To prepare the sardines, cut off the fins
and remove the backbones, leaving the
heads and tails intact. • Wipe with damp
paper towels. • Arrange the fish in a
shallow baking dish and cover with the
onions, carrot, and parsley. • Mix the
vinegar, water, cinnamon, bay leaf,
peppercorns, thyme, salt, and oil in a
small bowl. Drizzle over the fish in the
dish. • Cover the dish with a lid or
aluminum foil. • Bake for 25 minutes.
• Let cool completely at room
temperature. • Set aside for several
hours before serving.

$1^1/_2$ **pounds (750 g)**
   fresh sardines

2 **onions, cut into**
   thin rings

1 **carrot, thinly sliced**
   lengthwise

1 **tablespoon finely**
   chopped fresh
   parsley

$^1/_2$ **cup (125 ml) white**
   wine vinegar

$^1/_2$ **cup (125 ml) water**

$^1/_4$ **teaspoon ground**
   cinnamon

1 **bay leaf**

6 **peppercorns**

1 **tablespoon fresh**
   thyme leaves

$^1/_2$ **teaspoon salt**

2 **tablespoons extra-**
   virgin olive oil

Serves: 6–8
Preparation: 20 minutes
   + several hours to
   gather flavor
Cooking: 25 minutes
Level: 2

■ ■ ■ *These sardines can be prepared a day or two*
ahead of serving and stored in the refrigerator.
They will only gain in flavor.

BESSARA

Place the fava beans in a large saucepan with the water, garlic, and onion. Bring to a boil and simmer until the beans are very soft, about 1 hour. • Transfer the beans, garlic, and onion to a food processor and purée until smooth, adding enough of the cooking water to make a smooth, thick dip. • Return the mixture to the saucepan. • Season with salt and stir in the olive oil, cumin, and paprika. • Cook over low heat until heated through, about 5 minutes. Add more cooking liquid if the mixture is too thick. • Pour into small bowls and garnish with the paprika and chives. • Serve as a dip with raw vegetables.

1	pound (500 g) dried fava (broad) beans, soaked overnight and drained
6	cups (1.5 liters) water
4	cloves garlic
1	onion, diced
	Salt
1/2	cup (125 ml) extra-virgin olive oil
2	teaspoons ground cumin
2	teaspoons hot paprika + extra, to dust
	Snipped chives, to serve
	Raw vegetables, such as celery and carrots, to serve

Serves: 8–10
Preparation: 15 minutes + 12 hours to soak the beans
Cooking: 65 minutes
Level: 1

■ ■ ■ *Serve this delicious Moroccan dip with fresh crusty bread or sliced carrots and celery to scoop it up. Set out small bowls of freshly squeezed lemon juice and extra-virgin olive oil to be added at will.*

POLENTA AND CORN FRITTERS

Bring the water and salt to a boil in a medium saucepan. • Gradually sprinkle in the polenta, stirring constantly with a wooden spoon to prevent lumps from forming. • Continue cooking, stirring almost constantly, until the polenta thickens, 8–10 minutes. • Remove from the heat and stir in the corn, scallions, parsley, and garlic. • Transfer to a bowl and let cool. • Sift the flour and baking soda into the polenta mixture. • Add the egg and season with salt and pepper. • Heat the oil in a large frying pan over medium-high heat and drop tablespoons of the mixture into the pan. • Fry until golden brown, 3–4 minutes each side. • Serve with the pesto crème fraîche.

■ ■ ■ *Pesto crème fraîche can be made by stirring 4–5 tablespoons of pesto (see Vegetable Lasagna with Pesto on page 226) into 1 cup (250 ml) of crème fraîche. If you don't have crème fraîche, mix ¹/₂ cup (125 ml) of sour cream with ¹/₂ cup (125 ml) of heavy (double) cream and chill for 2 hours in the refrigerator.*

1¹/₂ cups (375 ml) water

¹/₂ teaspoon salt

¹/₂ cup (85 g) instant polenta

1 cup (125 g) corn (sweet corn)

2 scallions (spring onions), thinly sliced

1 tablespoon finely chopped fresh parsley

1 small clove garlic, finely chopped

¹/₃ cup (50 g) all-purpose (plain) flour

¹/₄ teaspoon baking soda (bicarbonate of soda)

1 large egg, lightly beaten

Salt and freshly ground black pepper

¹/₄ cup (60 ml) extra-virgin olive oil

Pesto crème fraîche, to serve

Serves: 6–8
Preparation: 15 minutes
Cooking: 10 minutes
Level: 1

CRUMBED EGGPLANT

Place the eggplant in a colander and sprinkle with coarse sea salt. Let drain for 30 minutes. • Shake off excess salt. Pat dry with paper towels. • Beat the egg and milk in a small bowl until combined. • Chop the garlic and bread crumbs in a food processor. Place in a separate dish. • Dip the eggplant in the flour, then in the egg mixture, followed by the crumb mixture until well coated. • Heat the oil in a large, deep frying pan or deep-fryer over medium-high heat. • Fry the eggplant in 2–3 batches until golden brown, 5–7 minutes. • Drain on paper towels and sprinkle with the parsley. • Serve at once.

1 large eggplant (aubergine), cut crosswise into $^1/_2$-inch (1-cm) thick slices and quartered

1 tablespoon coarse sea salt

1 large egg

$^1/_2$ cup (125 ml) milk

2 cloves garlic

1 cup (125 g) fine dry bread crumbs

$^1/_3$ cup (50 g) all-purpose (plain) flour

4 cups (1 liter) olive oil, to deep fry

Coarsely chopped fresh parsley, to garnish

Serves: 4–6
Preparation: 10 minutes + 30 minutes to drain
Cooking: 10–20 minutes
Level: 2

BAKED RICOTTA MUSHROOMS

Preheat the oven to 350°F (180°C/gas 4).
• Line a baking sheet with parchment
paper. • Mix the ricotta, tomatoes, onion,
basil, chives, and lemon juice in a small
bowl. Season with pepper. • Spoon the
filling into the mushrooms and arrange
on the prepared baking sheet. • Sprinkle
the Parmesan and bread crumbs over the
mushrooms. • Bake for 10–15 minutes,
until golden. • Serve hot.

$1/2$ cup (125 g) fresh
ricotta cheese

3 sun-dried tomatoes,
soaked in warm
water until softened,
finely chopped

1 tablespoon finely
chopped onion

1 tablespoon finely
chopped fresh basil

1 tablespoon snipped
fresh chives

1 teaspoon freshly
squeezed lemon
juice

Freshly ground black
pepper

12 small mushroom
caps, stems
removed

2 tablespoons freshly
grated Parmesan

2 tablespoons fine dry
bread crumbs

Serves: 4–6
Preparation: 10 minutes
Cooking: 10–15 minutes
Level: 1

VEGETABLE TERRINE

Vegetable Terrine: Preheat the oven to 350°F (180°C/gas 4). • Line an 8 x 4-inch (10 x 20-cm) terrine mold or loaf pan with plastic wrap (cling film), leaving enough to hang over the sides to cover the top of the terrine. Set aside. • Cut the pumpkin into ½-inch (1-cm) thick slices to fit the shape of the mold. There should be enough for a single layer in the terrine. • Arrange the pumpkin on a baking sheet and brush with oil. • Bake for 25–30 minutes, until cooked, but still firm. • Cut the tomatoes in half lengthwise. Remove the seeds and flatten them slightly. • Cut the cheese into ¼-inch (5-mm) thick slices. • Heat a grill pan and grill the zucchini until tender, 3–5 minutes. • Layer the ingredients in the mold in the following order: tomatoes, basil, mozzarella, pumpkin, zucchini, mozzarella, basil, tomatoes, and zucchini. The overall effect should be layers of tomatoes, basil, and

Vegetable Terrine

12 ounces (350 g) pumpkin or winter squash, peeled

16 plum tomatoes

1 medium zucchini (courgette), thinly sliced lengthwise

14 ounces (400 g) fresh mozzarella cheese, drained

1 bunch fresh basil

Freshly ground black pepper

Mustard and Balsamic Dressing

1 teaspoon whole-grain mustard

2 tablespoons balsamic vinegar

¼ cup (60 ml) extra-virgin olive oil

Serves: 8–10
Preparation: 25 minutes + 12 hours to chill
Cooking: 25–30 minutes
Level: 3

cheese with a layer of pumpkin in the center. When layering, place the tomatoes skin-side down and season each tomato layer with a little pepper. Cover the terrine with the overhanging plastic wrap. Place a plate on top to weigh it down and chill overnight.

Mustard and Balsamic Dressing: Whisk the mustard, vinegar, and oil in a small bowl until well combined. Set aside until ready to use. • Use the plastic wrap to carefully lift the terrine out of the mold and cut into thick slices. • Arrange on serving plates and drizzle with the dressing.

See photograph on the following page

CAMEMBERT PARCELS

Lay out a sheet of phyllo pastry on a work surface and brush lightly with butter. • Take a second sheet and place it on top of the first sheet at an angle to form a star shape with eight points. Brush with butter. • Take a third sheet and place again at an angle to add four more points to the star shape. Brush with butter. • Sprinkle a little rosemary over the pastry and place the Camembert in the center. Season with pepper • Bring the edges of the pastry up over the cheese and scrunch together to close at the top. Brush with butter. Repeat for the other parcels. • Cover loosely with plastic wrap (cling film) and chill for 2 hours. • Preheat the oven to 400°F (200°C/ gas 6). • Butter a large baking sheet. • Arrange the parcels on the prepared sheet. • Bake for 25 minutes, or until crisp and golden. • Let cool for 15 minutes. • Cut each parcel into quarters and serve warm, sprinkled with extra rosemary.

9   **sheets phyllo pastry, cut into 12-inch (30-cm) squares**

2/3   **cup (150 g) butter, melted**

3   **tablespoons finely chopped fresh rosemary, + extra to garnish**

3   **(8-ounce/250-g) round Camembert cheeses**

    Freshly ground black pepper

Serves: 6–12
Preparation: 20 minutes + 2 hours to chill
Cooking: 25 minutes
Level: 2

BRUSCHETTA WITH MOZZARELLA AND BASIL

44

Preheat the broiler (grill). • Toast the bread on each side for 2–3 minutes until lightly browned. • Brush with the oil and spread with the sun-dried tomato paste. • Top with the mozzarella, tomatoes, and basil. Season with pepper. • Serve at once.

1   ciabatta loaf, cut into 1-inch (2-cm) slices

1/4 cup (60 ml) extra-virgin olive oil

1/3 cup (90 ml) sun-dried tomato pesto (see page 160)

6   ounces (180 g) mozzarella bocconcini, each cut into 5 slices

12 ounces (350 g) cherry tomatoes, cut in half

3   tablespoons shredded basil

Freshly ground black pepper

Serves: 6–8
Preparation: 10 minutes
Cooking: 5–6 minutes
Level: 1

TIROPETES

Preheat the oven to 400°F (200°C/ gas 6). • Mix the ricotta, feta, and eggs in a medium bowl. Season with pepper. • Brush one sheet of phyllo pastry with melted butter and place another sheet on top. Cut the pastry lengthwise into four strips. • To shape the triangles, place a heaped teaspoon of the cheese mixture close to the bottom of the right-hand corner of the strip. Fold this corner over the mixture diagonally across to the left-hand edge to form a triangle. Continue folding from right to left in a triangular shape to the end of the strip. • Brush the top of the triangle with melted butter and arrange on a baking sheet. • Repeat until all mixture has been used. • Bake for about 20 minutes, or until golden. • Serve at once.

1¼ cups (300 g) fresh ricotta cheese

12 ounces (350 g) feta cheese, crumbled

4 large eggs, lightly beaten

Freshly ground white pepper

1 16-ounce (500-g) packet phyllo pastry

½ cup (125 g) butter, melted

Serves: 12–14
Preparation: 25 minutes
Cooking: 20 minutes
Level: 3

■ ■ ■ *Tiropetes are a delicious type of Greek finger food made of cheese-filled triangles of phyllo pastry brushed with butter.*

ASPARAGUS PARMESAN PASTRY SPIRALS

Preheat the oven to 425°F (220°C/gas 7).
• Line a baking sheet with parchment
paper. • Mix the Parmesan, lemon zest,
pepper, and paprika in a small bowl.
• Lay out a sheet of phyllo pastry on a
work surface. Fold in half lengthwise.
• Lightly brush with oil. Sprinkle with
one-sixth of the Parmesan mixture. Cut
in half lengthwise. • Wrap a slice of ham
around an asparagus spear. • Place a
pastry strip around the spear, winding in
a spiral from the bottom. • Arrange on
the prepared baking sheet. • Repeat with
remaining ingredients to make 12 spirals.
Dust lightly with paprika. • Bake until
golden, 10–12 minutes. • Serve with
balsamic vinegar for dipping.

2   tablespoons freshly
    grated Parmesan
    cheese

2   teaspoons finely
    grated lemon zest

1   teaspoon freshly
    ground black pepper

1   teaspoon sweet
    paprika + extra,
    to dust

6   sheets phyllo pastry

12 slices turkey ham

12 asparagus spears,
    wooden ends
    removed

    Balsamic vinegar,
    to serve

Serves: 4–6
Preparation: 15 minutes
Cooking: 10–12 minutes
Level: 2

TERRINE OF LEEK AND ROASTED BELL PEPPERS

Broil (grill) the bell peppers until the skins are blackened all over. • Wrap them in a paper bag for 10 minutes, then remove the skins and seeds. Slice into lengths and set aside. • Slice the leek in half lengthwise and separate the leaves. Rinse under cold running water to remove any dirt. • Blanch the leek leaves in a large pot of boiling water for 3 minutes. • Drain and plunge in cold water. • Line a 8 x 4-inch (10 x 20-cm) loaf pan with plastic wrap (cling film). • Drape the cooked leek leaves over the bottom and sides of the pan, allowing the long ends to hang over the sides. • Sauté the scallions in the butter in a small frying pan over medium heat until softened, about 3 minutes. • Mix the scallions, cream cheese, goat cheese, parsley, and basil in a large bowl. Season with salt and pepper. • Sprinkle the gelatin into the cold water and let soak for 1 minute. • Place the gelatin mixture

2	red bell peppers (capsicums)
2	yellow bell peppers (capsicums)
1	large leek
1	bunch scallions (spring onions), sliced
1/4	cup (60 g) butter
2/3	cup (150 g) cream cheese
1 1/4	cups (300 g) chèvre or other fresh goat cheese, softened
3	tablespoons finely chopped fresh parsley
20	fresh basil leaves, torn
	Salt and freshly ground black pepper
2	teaspoons plain gelatin
1	tablespoon cold water
1 1/4	cups (300 ml) heavy (double) cream

Serves: 8–10
Preparation: 40 minutes + 12 hours to chill
Cooking: 30 minutes
Level: 3

in a microwave and heat for 20 seconds on medium until the mixture is boiling (or heat in a small saucepan until boiling). • Stir well with a fork. • Add the gelatin and cream to the cheese mixture and mix well. • Pour one-third of the cheese mixture into the prepared loaf pan and cover with yellow bell pepper slices. • Cover with another third of the cheese mixture, topping with a layer of red bell pepper. • Finish with the remaining cheese mixture and drape the leeks hanging over the sides over the cheese filling. (Use any leftover leeks to fill in the gaps if necessary.) • Chill overnight. • Use the plastic wrap to carefully lift the terrine out of the mold and cut into thick slices.

See photograph on the following page

GOAT CHEESE AND ZUCCHINI RICE FRITTERS

Place rice and 2 cups (500 ml) of water in a large saucepan and bring to a boil. Reduce the heat to low, cover, and simmer until tender, about 15 minutes. • Remove from heat, and let stand, covered, for 5 more minutes. • Combine the cooked rice, onion, parsley, zucchini, Fontina, goat cheese, eggs, flour, and seasoning and stir to combine. Refrigerate for 20 minutes. • Heat the oil in a large heavy frying pan. Add tablespoon-size scoops of the mixture and fry until golden, 2–3 minutes each side. Drain on paper towels. • Serve hot with the salsa passed separately.

■ ■ ■ *The Italian salsa that accompanies these fritters is similar to a Mexican salsa. In both Italian and Spanish,* salsa *means "sauce."*

1 cup (200 g) long-grain rice

1 large onion, chopped

3 tablespoons finely chopped fresh parsley

2 large zucchini (courgettes), grated

1 1/2 ounces (45 g) Fontina cheese, grated

3 ounces (90 g) chèvre or other fresh soft goat cheese

2 large eggs

2 tablespoons all-purpose (plain) flour

Salt and freshly ground black pepper

2 tablespoons extra-virgin olive oil

Tomato Salsa (see Stuffed Zucchini with Tomato and Pecorino, page 290)

Serves: 4
Preparation: 10 minutes
Cooking: 30 minutes
Level: 2

DEEP-FRIED CRAB BALLS

Tartar Sauce: Combine all ingredients in a bowl and refrigerate until ready to use.
Crab Balls: Combine the crab meat, butter, mustard, Tabasco, egg yolks and bread crumbs in a medium bowl. Mix well, seasoning with salt to taste. Cover and chill in the refrigerator until firm, at least 1 hour. • Shape into balls the size of small walnuts and return to the refrigerator for 30 minutes. • Roll the balls in the flour, shaking off excess. • Heat the oil in a large, deep frying pan or deep-fryer over medium-high heat. • Fry the crab balls until golden, 5–7 minutes. Scoop out with a slotted spoon and drain on paper towels. • Serve hot with the tartar sauce and a cucumber salad.

Tartar Sauce

1	cup (250 ml) mayonnaise
1	teaspoon finely chopped onion
1	teaspoon each finely chopped fresh parsley and basil
1	teaspoon finely chopped gherkins
1	teaspoon finely chopped green olives
1	teaspoon mustard
	Salt and pepper

Crab Balls

1	pound (500 g) crab-meat, flaked
1/4	cup (60 g) butter
1	tablespoon mustard
1/8	teaspoon Tabasco
2	large egg yolks
1/2	cup (30 g) fresh bread crumbs
	All-purpose (plain) flour
4	cups (1 liter) olive oil, to deep fry

Serve: 6–8
Preparation: 15 minutes + 90 minutes to chill
Cooking: 10 minutes
Level: 2

DOLMADES

Heat the oil in a large frying pan over medium heat and sauté the shallots and garlic until softened, about 5 minutes.
• Add the rice, golden raisins, pine nuts, and lemon juice and sauté for 1 minute. Season with salt and pepper, then add the water. • Cover the pan and simmer for 15 minutes, then turn off the heat and leave to cool. • Add the scallions, mint and parsley to the cooled mixture. • Rinse the vine leaves in cold water, then place them shiny side down on a work surface. Put 2–3 teaspoons of the stuffing on each leaf and roll into a tight parcel.
• Place the dolmades seam-side down in a steamer and steam until the leaves are tender, about 10 minutes. • Serve warm.

■ ■ ■ *Dolmades are vine leaves stuffed with a rice-, grain-, or meat-based filling. They are especially popular in Greece where they are usually served with tzatziki (see Tomatoes Filled with Tzatziki on page 86). Preserved grape leaves are found in jars wherever Middle Eastern foods are sold.*

1   tablespoon extra-virgin olive oil

3   shallots, finely chopped

2   cloves garlic, finely chopped

3/4 cup (150 g) short-grain rice

1/4 cup (50 g) golden raisins (sultanas)

1/4 cup (30 g) pine nuts, toasted

Freshly squeezed juice of 1 lemon

Salt and freshly ground black pepper

2/3 cup (150 ml) water

4   scallions (spring onions), finely chopped

1   tablespoon finely chopped fresh mint leaves and parsley

1   tablespoon finely chopped fresh parsley

20 preserved grape vine leaves

Serves: 4–6
Preparation: 30 minutes
Cooking: 5 minutes
Level: 1

ASPARAGUS WITH PECORINO AND PROSCIUTTO

Blanch the asparagus in a large saucepan of boiling water until tender, about 4 minutes depending on the thickness of the spears. • Drain and rinse in ice-cold water to stop the cooking process. Pat dry with paper towels. • Place the lemon juice in a small bowl. Slowly add the oil, whisking constantly, until the dressing thickens. Season with salt and pepper. • Wrap a slice of prosciutto around each asparagus spear and arrange on a serving dish. • Pour the dressing over the top and sprinkle with the pecorino cheese shavings. • Serve at once.

12 asparagus spears, tough woody ends removed

Freshly squeezed juice of 1 lemon

1/3 cup (90 ml) extra-virgin olive oil

Sea salt and freshly ground black pepper

6 large slices prosciutto, cut in half

Shavings of pecorino cheese

Serves: 4–6
Preparation: 10 minutes
Cooking: 4 minutes
Level: 2

SQUID WITH GARLIC AND CAPERS

Poaching Liquid: Combine the carrot, onion, thyme, garlic, water, lemon juice and zest, and capers in a medium saucepan. Bring to a boil and simmer for 10 minutes. • Add the squid and simmer until tender, 2–3 minutes. • Remove the garlic from the poaching liquid and slice.

Marinade: Combine the ingredients for the marinade in a medium bowl. Add the sliced garlic and mix together. • Remove the squid from the poaching liquid and cut into ¼-inch (5-mm) rings. • Transfer the squid to the marinade and chill for 30 minutes.

Salad: Mix the tomatoes in a bowl with the capers and parsley. • Remove the squid from the marinade and add to the salad. • Use ¼ cup (60 ml) of the marinade as a dressing. • Serve at once.

Poaching Liquid
1 carrot, chopped
1 onion, chopped
½ bunch thyme
8 cloves garlic
4 cups (1 liter) water
Juice and zest of 1 lemon
½ cup (50 g) capers
4 squid tubes, about 6 ounces (180 g) each

Marinade
1 teaspoon cumin
¾ cup (180 ml) extra-virgin olive oil
Juice of 2 lemons
1 teaspoon salt
½ teaspoon ground black pepper
8 sprigs lemon thyme

Salad
2 tomatoes, chopped
2 teaspoons capers
1 tablespoon finely chopped fresh parsley

Serves: 4–6
Preparation: 35 minutes + 30 minutes to chill
Cooking: 25–30 minutes
Level: 2

ARTICHOKE HEARTS STUFFED WITH TWO CHEESES

Preheat the broiler (grill). • Slice the bottoms off the artichoke hearts so they will stand upright. • Mix the ricotta, Parmesan, bell pepper, parsley, and pepper in a small bowl. • Spoon the mixture into the center of each artichoke heart. • Broil the artichokes about 5 inches (12 cm) from the heat source until the cheese begins to turn golden, 2–3 minutes. • Serve warm.

1 pound (500 g) jar or can artichoke hearts, drained

6 tablespoons ricotta cheese

3 tablespoons freshly grated Parmesan cheese

1 tablespoon diced red bell pepper (capsicum)

1 teaspoon finely chopped fresh parsley

1/2 teaspoon cracked pepper

Serves: 4–6
Preparation: 10 minutes
Cooking: 2–3 minutes
Level: 1

SPINACH TARTS

Pastry Shells: Process the flour, Parmesan, and butter in a food processor until the mixture resembles fine bread crumbs.
• With the motor running, slowly add enough water to form a soft dough. • Shape the dough into a ball. Wrap in plastic wrap (cling film) and chill for 30 minutes.
• Preheat the oven to 350°F (180°C/gas 4)
• Roll out the pastry to $1/8$ inch (3 mm) thick. Use a $3^1/2$-inch (8-cm) fluted pastry cutter to cut out twenty pastry rounds.
• Arrange the pastry rounds in tartlet pans.
• Prick the bottoms and sides of the pastry with a fork. • Bake for 5–10 minutes, until lightly golden.
Filling: Sauté the scallions, spinach, and garlic in the oil in a medium frying pan over medium heat until the spinach has wilted.
• Remove from the heat and set aside to cool. • Mix the spinach mixture, ricotta, eggs, milk, and nutmeg in a medium bowl.
• Spoon the filling evenly into the pastry shells. • Bake for 15–20 minutes, until golden brown. • Serve warm.

Pastry Shells

$1^1/4$ cups (180 g) all-purpose (plain) flour

$1/4$ cup (30 g) freshly grated Parmesan cheese

Scant $1/2$ cup (100 g) butter, cut up

3 tablespoons ice water

Filling

2 scallions (spring onions), finely chopped

8 spinach leaves, finely shredded

1 clove garlic, finely chopped

2 teaspoons extra-virgin olive oil

$1/2$ cup (125 g) ricotta cheese, drained

2 large eggs, lightly beaten

$1/3$ cup (90 ml) milk

$1/2$ teaspoon nutmeg

Serves: 8–10
Preparation: 45 minutes + 30 minutes to chill
Cooking: 25–35 minutes
Level: 2

FETA, OLIVE, AND BELL PEPPER TARTLETS

Preheat the oven to 400°F (200°C/ gas 6). • Set out a 6-cup muffin pan. • Use a pastry cutter to cut out six rounds from the pastry large enough to line the base and sides of the muffin cups (about 4 inches/10 cm in diameter). • Arrange the pastry rounds in the muffin cups, making sure that the pastry slightly overlaps the tops. • Mix the feta, olives, bell pepper, basil, and eggs in a small bowl. Season with pepper. • Spoon the mixture evenly into the shells. • Bake for 15–20 minutes, until the pastry is golden brown and the filling is set. • Serve warm.

1   15-ounce (500-g) package short-crust pastry

4   ounces (125 g) feta cheese, crumbled

1/4 cup (25 g) Kalamata olives, thinly sliced

1/2 red bell pepper (capsicum), thinly sliced

2   basil leaves, torn

2   large eggs, lightly beaten

    Freshly ground black pepper

Serves: 4
Preparation: 15 minutes
Cooking: 15–20 minutes
Level: 2

RED ONIONS MARINATED IN BALSAMIC VINEGAR

Preheat the oven to 375°F (190°C/gas 5). • Use a sharp knife to cut a thin slice off the bottom of each onion so that it will sit upright. • Cut a thin slice from the top of each onion and then cut small slits deep in the center. Insert two rosemary sprigs and several garlic slivers into each onion. • Arrange the onions in a small baking dish. • Mix the stock, oil, balsamic vinegar, red wine vinegar, and brown sugar in a small bowl. • Pour this mixture over the onions. • Bake for 1 hour (basting a few times with the onion juices) until the onions are softened when pierced with a sharp knife. • Just before serving, split the skins with a sharp knife and remove. Season the onions with salt and pepper. • Serve hot.

8   medium red onions

8   sprigs rosemary

6   cloves garlic, thinly sliced

3/4   cup (180 ml) vegetable stock (see page 251)

1/4   cup (60 ml) extra-virgin olive oil

2   tablespoons balsamic vinegar

2   tablespoons red wine vinegar

1   tablespoon brown sugar

    Salt and freshly ground black pepper

Serves: 8
Preparation: 30 minutes
Cooking: 1 hour
Level: 2

MARINATED BELL PEPPERS

Broil (grill) the bell peppers until the skins are blackened all over. • Wrap them in a paper bag for 10 minutes, then remove the skins and seeds. Slice into lengths and place in a shallow dish.
• Add the capers, garlic, oil, sumac, vinegar, and paprika and mix well.
• Cover with plastic wrap (cling film) and chill for at least 2 hours. • Serve hot or cold. Heat in a warm oven for 6–8 minutes if serving hot.

4	red or yellow bell peppers (capsicums)
1	tablespoon capers, soaked in salted water before use
1	clove garlic, finely chopped
3	tablespoons extra-virgin olive oil
1/2	teaspoon sumac or lemon zest
2	tablespoons balsamic vinegar
1/2	teaspoon smoked sweet paprika

Serves: 4–6
Preparation: 30 minutes
  + 2 hours to chill
Cooking: 20 minutes
Level: 2

■ ■ ■ *Sumac is a spice made from the berries of a bush that grows wild in Sicily, southern Italy, and parts of the Middle East. It also grows wild in the United States but must be distinguished from its toxic white-berried cousin. It is safest to buy the spice at a Middle Eastern food market.*

SMELT FRITTERS

Mix the smelts, shallots, dill, lemon zest and juice, flour, and eggs in a large bowl until well combined. • Season with salt and pepper. • Heat the oil in a large, deep frying pan or deep-fryer until very hot. • Drop tablespoons of the mixture into the pan and fry for 2–3 minutes until golden brown. • Serve hot with lemon wedges.

1	pound (500 g) smelts of whitebait
2	shallots, finely sliced
2	teaspoons finely chopped fresh dill
	Finely grated zest of 2 lemons
2	teaspoons freshly squeezed lemon juice
1/2	cup (75 g) all-purpose (plain) flour
2	large eggs, lightly beaten
	Salt and freshly ground black pepper
	Olive oil, for frying
	Lemon wedges, to serve

Serves: 4–6
Preparation: 10 minutes
Cooking: 10 minutes
Level: 1

MARINATED MUSHROOMS

Mix the oil, lemon juice, thyme, fennel, garlic, celery, peppercorns, bay leaf, and water in a medium saucepan and bring to a boil over medium heat. • Cover, decrease the heat, and simmer for 3 minutes until the celery is just tender • Trim off the mushroom stems. • Cut the lemon in half and run the cut surface of the lemon over the mushrooms. • Add the mushroom caps to the simmering liquid and cook for 5 minutes. • Remove the mushrooms with a slotted spoon and place on a serving dish. • Turn up the heat and boil the liquid until it has reduced and thickened. Pour the sauce over the mushrooms. • Let cool completely. • Cover with plastic wrap (cling film) and chill for at least 1 hour before serving.

$1/2$ **cup (125 ml) extra-virgin olive oil**

$1/3$ **cup (90 ml) freshly squeezed lemon juice**

2 **sprigs fresh thyme**

1 **stalk fennel**

1 **clove garlic, finely chopped**

1 **stalk celery, finely chopped**

10 **black peppercorns**

1 **bay leaf**

$1/2$ **cup (125 ml) water**

2 **pounds (1 kg) button mushrooms**

1 **lemon**

Serves: 8–12
Preparation: 20 minutes + 1 hour to chill
Cooking: 15 minutes
Level: 2

GREEK LAMB KEBABS

Mix lamb, bread crumbs, garlic, onion, cumin, parsley, mint, oregano, lemon zest, and egg in a large bowl. Season with salt and pepper. • Roll the mixture into sausage shapes and thread onto eight bamboo or metal skewers. • Arrange the kebabs on a tray and chill overnight in the refrigerator. • Oil the grill rack or grill pan and cook the kebabs for 5 minutes, turning frequently. • Serve hot with the tzatziki.

12	ounces (350 g) ground (minced) lamb
1	cup (60 g) fresh bread crumbs
1	clove garlic, finely chopped
1	small onion, finely chopped
1	teaspoon ground cumin
1	tablespoon finely chopped fresh parsley
1	tablespoon finely chopped fresh mint
1	teaspoon finely chopped fresh oregano
	Finely grated zest of 1 lemon
1	large egg
	Salt and freshly ground black pepper
	Tzatziki (see Tomatoes Filled with Tzatziki, page 86), to serve

■ ■ ■ These kebabs make wonderful barbecue food. They can be prepared the day before and chilled until just before cooking. If using bamboo skewers, be sure to soak them in cold water for about 30 minutes before use so that they don't burn during cooking.

Serves: 4–8
Preparation: 50 minutes + overnight to chill
Cooking: 5 minutes
Level: 2

OLIVE TAPENADE

Combine the olives, parsley, garlic, capers, shallot, lemon juice, and oregano in a food processor and process until well combined. • With the motor running, add the oil in a slow stream and process until a paste has formed. • Season with salt and pepper. • Spread the tapenade over the slices of bread and serve.

1   cup (125 g) black olives, pitted

1/2 cup (20 g) fresh parsley

2   cloves garlic

1   tablespoon capers

1   shallot, thinly sliced

2   tablespoons freshly squeezed lemon juice

2   teaspoons finely chopped fresh oregano

1/3 cup (90 ml) extra-virgin olive oil

Salt and freshly ground black pepper

1   loaf French bread, thickly sliced, toasted

Serves: 4
Preparation: 10 minutes
Level: 1

CHEESE AND SESAME PUFFS

Mix the flour, baking powder, and paprika into a medium bowl. • Add the eggs, one at a time, mixing until just combined. • Stir in the cheese and ham. • Season with salt and pepper. • Shape the mixture into small balls the size of small plums. • Chill for at least 4 hours. • Roll the balls in the sesame seeds. • Heat the oil in a deep-fryer or large, deep frying pan to very hot. • Fry the balls in batches until puffed and golden brown, 5–7 minutes per batch. • Drain on paper towels and serve hot.

$1/2$ cup (75 g) all-purpose (plain) flour

$1/2$ teaspoon baking powder

$1/2$ teaspoon sweet paprika

2 large eggs, lightly beaten

1 cup (125 g) finely grated firm-textured cheese, such as Fontina or Cheddar

$1/2$ cup (60 g) diced ham

Salt and freshly ground black pepper

6 tablespoons sesame seeds, toasted

4 cups (1 liter) olive oil, for frying

Serves: 4–6
Preparation: 20 minutes
  + 4 hours to chill
Cooking: 20 minutes
Level: 1

TARAMASALATA

Combine the potatoes, roe, onion, oil, and lemon juice in a food processor and pulse until smooth. Add more oil if the dip is too thick. • Season with salt and pepper. • Transfer to a serving bowl, cover with plastic wrap (cling film) and chill for at least 2 hours before serving. • Serve with the olives and pita bread.

2   **medium potatoes, peeled and boiled**

5   **ounces (150 g) cod roe or carp roe**

1   **small onion, finely chopped**

2/3 **cup (150 ml) extra-virgin olive oil**

Freshly squeezed juice of 1 lemon

Salt and freshly ground black pepper

Black olives, to serve

Pita bread, to serve

Serves: 6–8
Preparation: 15 minutes
 + 2 hours to chill
Level: 1

■ ■ ■ *Taramasalata, or cod roe dip, is a classic Greek appetizer. Serve it with crackers and sliced vegetables with predinner drinks, or as part of a spread of an eye-catching meze at the beginning of a meal. Look for the fish roe, sometimes called "tarama," wherever Greek foods are sold.*

TOMATOES FILLED WITH TZATZIKI

Tomatoes: Slice the tops off the tomatoes. Carefully scoop out the flesh and seeds. Sprinkle the insides with salt. • Drain the tomatoes cut-side down on paper towels for 30 minutes.

Tzatziki: Peel the cucumber. Cut it in half and scoop out the seeds. Cut into very small dice. Sprinkle with salt and drain in a colander for 10 minutes. • Squeeze out the excess moisture. • Mix the yogurt, garlic, cucumber, and mint in a large bowl. • Stir in the oil and vinegar and season with salt and pepper. • Spoon the mixture into the tomatoes. • Chill in the refrigerator for at least 1 hour before serving.

Tomatoes

12	small ripe tomatoes
	Salt and freshly ground black pepper

Tzatziki

1	cucumber
1	cup (250 ml) thick Greek-style yogurt
2	cloves garlic, finely chopped
1	bunch fresh mint, finely chopped
2	tablespoons extra-virgin olive oil
1	tablespoon white wine vinegar
	Salt and freshly ground black pepper

Serves: 4–6
Preparation: 25 minutes
 + 1 hour 30 minutes
 to drain and chill
Level: 2

■ ■ ■ *Tzatziki is a classic meze (appetizer) and also a side for meat dishes in Greek and many other cuisines of the eastern Mediterranean.*

SHRIMP VOL-AU-VENTS

Preheat the oven to 400°F (200°C/ gas 6). • Bring a small pan of salted water to a boil over medium-high heat. • Blanch the shrimp for 1 minute. Drain and let cool. • Melt the butter in a small saucepan over low heat. • Add the flour and cook over low heat for 2 minutes, stirring constantly. • Remove from the heat and pour in the milk all at once. • Place over a slightly higher heat and cook until thickened, stirring constantly. • Remove from the heat and stir in the lemon juice, chives, and paprika. Season with salt and pepper. • Fill the pastry shells with the mixture and arrange a shrimp on top of each one. • Place on a lightly greased baking sheet. • Bake for about 10 minutes, or until the pastry is golden brown. • Garnish with the chives. • Serve hot or at room temperature.

18   **medium shrimp (prawn) tails, peeled and deveined**

2   **tablespoons butter**

3   **tablespoons all-purpose (plain) flour**

1   **cup (250 ml) milk**

    Few drops freshly squeezed lemon juice

1   **tablespoon finely chopped fresh chives**

1   **teaspoon sweet paprika**

    Salt and freshly ground black pepper

18   **vol-au-vent or puff pastry shells, thawed, if frozen**

    Short lengths of chives, to garnish

Serves: 6–9
Preparation: 20 minutes
Cooking: 20 minutes
Level: 2

BAKED FIGS WRAPPED IN PANCETTA

90

Preheat the oven to 300°F (150°C/gas 2). • Wrap each fig in a slice of pancetta and secure with toothpicks onto which a bay leaf has been threaded. • Arrange the figs in a nonstick baking dish. • Bake until the figs are pink and a thick liquid has formed, about 20 minutes. • Transfer to serving dishes and pour the cooking juices over the top. • Serve hot.

12 ripe figs
12 slices pancetta
12 bay leaves

Serves: 4
Preparation: 10 minutes
Cooking: 20 minutes
Level: 1

GRAPE BITES

Chop the garlic, sage, and the leaves of 1 sprig of rosemary. • Mix the pork, chopped herbs, and fennel seeds in a large bowl. Season with salt and pepper. • Wash and dry the grapes. Carefully peel each one. • Shape the pork mixture into small balls the size of walnuts. Make a hollow in the center and place a grape in the center. Close up the meatball. • Finely chop the remaining rosemary leaves and mix with the bread crumbs. • Roll the meatballs in the mixture until well coated. • Heat the oil in a deep-fryer or large, deep frying pan to very hot. • Fry the meatballs in batches until golden brown, 5–7 minutes per batch. • Drain well on paper towels. • Serve hot.

1   **clove garlic**
2   **leaves sage**
2   **sprigs rosemary**
1   **pound (500 g) ground (minced) pork**
$1/2$ **teaspoon crushed fennel seeds**
  Salt and freshly ground black pepper
  16 large seedless green grapes
$2/3$ **cup (100 g) fine dry bread crumbs**
4   **cups (1 liter) olive oil, for frying**

Serves: 4–6
Preparation: 20 minutes
Cooking: 20 minutes
Level: 2

SWEET POTATO AND CANNELLINI FALAFEL

Boil (or microwave) the sweet potato until tender. Mash in a medium bowl, and set aside. • Sauté the garlic, cumin, and coriander in the oil in a large frying pan over medium heat for 1–2 minutes. • Stir in the tomato paste and cook until it turns a deep red and develops a rich aroma, 3–4 minutes. • Transfer the mixture to a food processor. • Add beans, cilantro, tahini, and lemon juice and process to make a rough paste. • Add the bean mixture and bread crumbs to the mashed sweet potato. Mix well. • Shape the mixture into small 1-inch (2.5 cm) patties. • Dip in the flour to coat, shaking to remove the excess. • Arrange on a plate and cover with plastic wrap (cling film). • Chill for at least 30 minutes or until ready to cook. The patties can be made up to this stage a day in advance. • Heat the oil in a deep-fryer or large, deep frying pan to very hot. • Fry the falafel in batches until golden brown, 5–7 minutes per batch. • Drain well on paper towels. • Serve hot.

1   pound (500 g) sweet potato, peeled and cut into chunks

1   clove garlic, finely chopped

2   teaspoons ground cumin

1   teaspoon ground coriander

2   teaspoons extra-virgin olive oil

1   tablespoon tomato paste (concentrate)

1   (14-ounce/400-g) can cannellini beans, drained

2   tablespoons fresh cilantro (coriander)

1   tablespoon tahini (sesame seed paste)

1   tablespoon lemon juice

1   cup (60 g) fresh bread crumbs

1   cup (150 g) all-purpose (plain) flour

4   cups (1 liter) olive oil, for frying

    Store-bought hummus, to serve

Serves: 6
Preparation: 30 minutes + 30 minutes to chill
Cooking: 25 minutes
Level: 2

FALAFEL

Soak the beans in a large bowl of cold water for 24 hours. • Drain well and process with the onion, garlic, potato, and parsley in a food processor until coarsely chopped. • Add the coriander, cumin, and flour, and process until well blended. • Season with salt and pepper. • Let rest for 2 hours. • Stir the baking powder into the mixture and shape into flattened patties. • Heat the oil in a deep-fryer or large, deep frying pan to very hot. • Fry the patties in batches until golden brown, 5–7 minutes per batch. • Drain well and pat dry on paper towels. • Serve warm with pita bread, tzatziki, tomatoes, and lettuce.

1	pound (500 g) dried white fava (broad) beans, soaked and drained
1	medium onion
3	cloves garlic
1	potato, peeled
1	bunch fresh parsley
1	teaspoon ground coriander
1	teaspoon ground cumin
2	tablespoons all-purpose (plain) flour
	Salt and freshly ground black pepper
1	teaspoon baking powder
4	cups (1 liter) olive oil, for frying
	Tzatziki (see Tomatoes Filled with Tzatziki, page 86), to serve
	Pita bread, to serve
	Lettuce and tomatoes, to serve

Serves: 4–6
Preparation: 30 minutes
  + 24 hours to soak
  + 2 hours to rest
Cooking: 20 minutes
Level: 2

■ ■ ■ *White fava beans, also called broad beans, are available in many Greek or Mediterranean specialty stores. If you can't find them, substitute with the same quantity of garbanzo beans (chickpeas).*

BREADS

ONION AND SAGE FOCACCIA

Basic Dough: Place the yeast in a small bowl. Add ¼ cup (60 ml) of the warm water and stir until dissolved. Set aside until frothy, 5–10 minutes. • Combine the flour and salt in a large bowl. Pour in the yeast mixture and enough of the remaining water to create a soft dough. • Transfer to a floured work surface and knead until smooth and elastic, about 10 minutes.
• Shape into a ball and place in a clean, lightly oiled bowl. Let rise until doubled in bulk, about 1½ hours.

Topping: Spread the onions out on a baking sheet, sprinkle with the salt, and let rest for 1 hour. • Shake off excess salt. • Oil a large baking pan (a 10 x 15-inch/25 x 38-cm jelly-roll pan is ideal). • Place the dough in the pan and use your fingertips to spread.
• Top with the onions and sage. Drizzle with the oil. • Let rise for 30 minutes. • Preheat the oven to 400°F (200°C/gas 6). • Bake until golden brown, about 25 minutes.
• Serve hot or at room temperature.

Basic Dough

2 (¼-ounce/7-g) packages active dry yeast or 1 ounce (25 g) compressed fresh yeast

About 1¼ cups (300 ml) warm water

3⅓ cups (500 g) all-purpose (plain) flour

½ teaspoon salt

Topping

3 large white onions, thinly sliced

½ teaspoon salt

15 leaves fresh sage

¼ cup (60 ml) extra-virgin olive oil

Serves: 4–6
Preparation: 45 minutes + 2 hours to rise
Cooking: 25 minutes
Level: 1

POTATO FOCACCIA WITH CHERRY TOMATOES

Cook the potato in a small pot of salted boiling water until tender, about 10 minutes. Drain and mash until smooth.
• Prepare the basic dough. Gradually work the mashed potato and 2 tablespoons of oil into the dough as you knead. Let rise in a warm place until doubled in volume, about 1½ hours.
• Oil a large baking pan (a 10 x 15-inch/ 25 x 38-cm jelly-roll pan is ideal). • Place the dough in the pan and use your fingertips to spread evenly. • Press the tomatoes lightly into the dough, cut-side up, and sprinkle with the sea salt and oregano. Drizzle with the remaining oil and let rise for 30 minutes. • Preheat the oven to 400°F (200°C/gas 6). • Bake until golden brown, 25–30 minutes.
• Serve hot or at room temperature.

1   large baking (floury) potato, peeled and cut into small cubes

Basic Dough (see Onion and Sage Focaccia, page 100

¼   cup (60 ml) extra-virgin olive oil

20 cherry tomatoes, cut in half

1   teaspoon coarse sea salt

1   tablespoon finely chopped fresh oregano or 1 teaspoon dried oregano

Serves: 4–6
Preparation: 45 minutes + 2 hours to rise
Cooking: 25–30 minutes
Level: 1

FILLED FOCACCIA WITH ZUCCHINI

Prepare the basic dough. Gradually work the oil, lard, and 1 tablespoon of rosemary into the dough as you knead. Let rise in a warm place until doubled in bulk, about 1$\frac{1}{2}$ hours. • Preheat a grill pan or griddle over medium heat. Grill the zucchini on both sides until tender and lightly browned. • Oil a 9-inch (23-cm) square baking pan. • Divide the dough half. Press one half into the bottom and up the sides of the prepared pan. • Cover with the mozzarella and zucchini. Season with salt and pepper. • Roll out the remaining dough on a lightly floured work surface until large enough to cover the pan. Place over the filling. Press the edges together to seal. Prick well with a fork. Let rise for 30 minutes. • Preheat the oven to 425°F (220°C/gas 7). • Brush the focaccia with the remaining oil. Spread the tomato on top. Sprinkle with the remaining rosemary and season with salt. • Bake until golden brown, 25–30 minutes. • Serve hot.

Basic Dough (see Onion and Sage Focaccia, page 100)

2 tablespoons extra-virgin olive oil

2 tablespoons lard, melted

2 tablespoons fresh rosemary leaves

3 medium zucchini (courgettes), sliced thinly lengthwise

8 ounces (250 g) mozzarella cheese, shredded or cut into small cubes

Salt and freshly ground black pepper

1 tomato, very thinly sliced

Serves: 4–6
Preparation: 45 minutes + 2 hours to rise
Cooking: 30–35 minutes
Level: 1

BELL PEPPER AND ONION FOCACCIA

Prepare the basic dough. Let rise in a warm place until doubled in bulk, about 1½ hours. • Heat 3 tablespoons of the oil in a large frying pan over medium-low heat. Add the onions, bell peppers, and parsley and simmer, stirring occasionally, until the vegetables are soft but not browned, 20–25 minutes. Add a few tablespoons of water, if necessary, to prevent browning. Season with salt and pepper. • Preheat the oven to 400°F (200°C/gas 6). • Oil a large baking pan (a 10 x 15-inch/25 x 38-cm jelly-roll pan is ideal). • Place the dough in the pan and use your fingertips to spread evenly. • Spread the vegetable mixture over dough and arrange the anchovy fillets on top. Drizzle with the remaining oil. • Bake until golden brown, 25–30 minutes. • Serve hot.

Basic Dough (see Onion and Sage Focaccia, page 100

¼ cup (60 ml) extra-virgin olive oil

1 pound (500 g) mild red or yellow onions, halved and sliced

2 red bell peppers (capsicums), sliced

2 green bell peppers (capsicums), sliced

2 tablespoons finely chopped fresh parsley

Salt and freshly ground black pepper

12 anchovy fillets, drained

Serves: 4–6
Preparation: 30 minutes
+ 1 hour 30 minutes
to rise
Cooking: 45–55 minutes
Level: 1

FRENCH SOURDOUGH WITH CARAMELIZED ONIONS

Starter: Combine the flour, yogurt, sugar, yeast, and water in a medium bowl. Mix well. Let rest for 24 hours.

Dough: Next day, melt the butter in large frying pan over medium heat. Add the onions and sauté until translucent. Cover the pan with a lid and simmer over low heat until golden brown, about 40 minutes.

• Mix the yeast, water, and sugar in a small bowl and let rest for 5 minutes. • Mix into the starter along with the salt, half the caramelized onions, and baking soda. Slowly add the flour until the dough is sticky but firm. You may not need all the flour.

• Knead for 10 minutes, then shape into a ball. Place in an oiled bowl and let rise for 30 minutes. • Divide the dough in half and shape each piece into a flat oval loaf about 1/2 inch (1 cm) thick. Top with the remaining onions and drizzle with the oil. Let rise for 1 hour. • Preheat the oven to 400°F (200°C /gas 6). • Bake 25–30 minutes, until crusty and golden brown.

Starter

1	cup (150 g) whole-wheat (wholemeal) flour
1	cup (250 ml) plain yogurt
1	teaspoon sugar
1	teaspoon active dry yeast
1/4	cup (60 ml) warm water

Dough

1/4	cup (60 g) butter
4	large onions, sliced
1	tablespoon active dry yeast
1/4	cup (60 ml) warm water
1	teaspoon sugar
1 1/2	teaspoons salt
1	teaspoon baking soda
3	cups (450 g) whole-wheat (wholemeal) flour
2	tablespoons extra-virgin olive oil

Serves: 8
Preparation: 1 hour
  + 25 hours to rise
Cooking: 65–75 minutes
Level: 3

CHEESE-FILLED FOCACCIA

Preheat the oven to 400°F (200°C/gas 6). • Oil a 9 x 13-inch (23 x 33-cm) baking pan. • Sift the flour and salt into a large bowl and make a well in the center. Stir in ¼ cup (60 ml) of oil and enough water to form a fairly soft dough. Divide in half and shape into two balls. Cover with a clean cloth and set aside to rest for 15 minutes. • Roll both pieces of dough out to fit the pan. Place one in the pan. Cover with the cheese, leaving a ½-inch (1-cm) border around the edges. Cover with the other piece of dough, pressing down to seal the edges. • Brush with the remaining 2 tablespoons oil of and sprinkle with the salt. • Bake for 15–20 minutes until lightly browned. If the dough puffs up while baking, prick with a fork.

3½ cups (500 g) all-purpose (plain) flour

1 teaspoon salt

¼ cup (60 ml) + 2 tablespoons extra-virgin olive oil

1 cup (250 ml) water

12 ounces (350 g) Gorgonzola or Taleggio cheese, melted with 1 tablespoon milk

1 teaspoon coarse sea salt, to sprinkle

Serves: 6
Preparation: 15 minutes
 + 15 minutes to rest
Cooking: 15–20 minutes
Level: 2

■■■ *This unleavened focaccia comes from Recco, near Genoa, in northeastern Italy. Try it with other fillings, but always use ingredients that cook quickly, such as sliced mushrooms or ham.*

ONION, BELL PEPPER, AND FETA PIZZA

Dough: Prepare the basic dough. Let rise in a warm place until doubled in bulk, about 1½ hours. • Oil two 12-inch (30-cm) pizza pans.

Topping: Heat the oil in a large frying pan over medium heat. Add the onions and sauté until softened, about 5 minutes. Reduce heat to low and simmer until caramelized, about 30 minutes. Remove from the heat and stir in the vinegar and basil. Season with black pepper. • Divide the dough in half and press into the prepared pans. Cover with clean kitchen towels and let rise in a warm place for 15 minutes. • Preheat the oven to 425°F (220°C/gas 7). • Spread the onions over the pizza dough. Top with bell peppers, feta, and olives. • Bake for 20–25 minutes until the crusts are crisp and golden. • Top with the arugula. Drizzle with extra balsamic vinegar, if liked. • Serve hot.

Basic Dough (see Onion and Sage Focaccia, page 100)

Topping

2 tablespoons extra-virgin olive oil

6 large mild red or yellow onions, thinly sliced

2 tablespoons balsamic vinegar + extra, to drizzle (optional)

¼ cup finely chopped fresh basil

Freshly ground black pepper

3 red bell peppers (capsicums), roasted, peeled, and sliced

5 ounces (150 g) feta cheese, crumbled

3 tablespoons sliced kalamata olives

1 bunch arugula (rocket)

Serves: 4–6
Preparation: 30 minutes + 1 hour 45 minutes to rise
Cooking: 55–60 minutes
Level: 2

SPICY PIZZAS WITH SPANISH ONION AND POTATO

Dough: Prepare the basic dough. Let rise in a warm place until doubled in bulk, about 1½ hours. • Oil two large baking sheets. • Preheat the oven to 450°F (225°C/gas 8). • Divide the dough into 8–12 pieces and spread each piece into a disk about 3 inches (8 cm) in diameter. Place the pizzas on the baking sheets.

Topping: Cover each pizza with some potato, onion, and rosemary, and drizzle with the chile oil. • Bake for 10–15 minutes until the crusts are golden brown and the potatoes are cooked. • Top with arugula and serve hot. Have extra chile oil on hand to drizzle.

Basic Dough (see Onion and sage Focaccia, page 100)

Topping
- 4 potatoes, very thinly sliced
- 2 small mild red or yellow onions, thinly sliced
- 3 sprigs rosemary, chopped
- ⅓ cup (90 ml) chile oil + extra, to serve (optional)
- Bunch of fresh arugula (rocket) leaves

Serves: 4–6
Preparation: 30 minutes + 1 hour 30 minutes to rise
Cooking: 10–15 minutes
Level: 1

■■■ *To vary the topping try sliced cherry tomatoes, arugula (rocket), and Parmesan flakes; or sun-dried tomatoes, bocconcini, and basil. Chile oil can be made at home easily by adding 4–6 small hot chiles to 2 cups (500 ml) of extra-virgin olive oil. Seal in a glass bottle or jar and leave to infuse for several days before use.*

PIZZA CAPRICCIOSA

Dough: Prepare the basic dough. Let rise in a warm place until doubled in bulk, about 1$\frac{1}{2}$ hours. • Oil two 12-inch (30-cm) pizza pans.

Topping: Heat $\frac{1}{4}$ cup (60 ml) of the oil in a medium saucepan over medium heat. Add the tomatoes and basil and simmer, stirring occasionally, until reduced a little, 10–15 minutes. Season with salt and pepper. • Divide the dough in half and press into the prepared pans. Cover with clean kitchen towels and let rise in a warm place for 15 minutes. • Preheat the oven to 400°F (200°C/gas 6). • Spread the sauce over the dough. Top with the artichokes, mushrooms, mozzarella, olives, and capers. Drizzle with the remaining 2 tablespoons oil. • Bake for 20–25 minutes until the crusts are crisp and golden. Serve hot.

Basic Dough (see Onion and sage Focaccia, page 100)

Topping

- $\frac{1}{4}$ **cup (60 ml) + 2 tablespoons extra-virgin olive oil**
- 2 **pounds (1 kg) tomatoes, peeled and chopped**
- 10 **fresh basil leaves**
  Salt and freshly ground black pepper
- 8 **ounces (250 g) canned artichoke hearts, drained and halved lengthwise**
- 12 **button mushrooms, finely sliced**
- 5 **ounces (150 g) mozzarella cheese, grated or sliced**
- 15 **black olives**
- 3 **tablespoons capers, drained**

Serves: 4–6
Preparation: 30 minutes + 1 hour 45 minutes to rise
Cooking: 35–40 minutes
Level: 1

FOUGASSE PROVENÇALE

Starter: Combine the yeast and water in a small bowl and let stand until frothy, 5–10 minutes. • Put the flour in a large bowl and stir in the yeast mixture. Cover the bowl with plastic wrap (cling film) and let stand at room temperature for 12–16 hours. It should first triple in bulk and then deflate. It will have a ripe, yeasty smell. **Dough:** Add the flour, salt, garlic (if using), oil, and enough water to the starter to make a soft dough. • Knead on a floured work surface until smooth and elastic. • Place in an oiled bowl and let rise until doubled in bulk, about 1 hour. • Knead again for 2–3 minutes. Return to the bowl and let rise until doubled in bulk, about 1 hour. • Divide the dough into 8–10 pieces and shape into ovals about 1/2 inch (1 cm) thick. Use a sharp knife to make diagonal cuts in the dough. Stretch to open up the holes. Brush with oil and sprinkle with sea salt. • Let rise for 30 minutes. • Preheat the oven to 400°F (200°C/gas 6). • Bake for about 25 minutes until golden brown.

Starter

1 (1/4-ounce/7-g) package active dry yeast or 1/2 ounce (15 g) fresh compressed yeast

3/4 cup (180 ml) warm water

1 1/2 cups (250 g) bread flour

Dough

1 1/2 cups (250 g) bread flour

1 teaspoon salt

2 cloves garlic, minced (optional)

1/3 cup (90 ml) warm water

2 tablespoons extra-virgin olive oil + extra, to brush

Coarse sea salt, to finish

Serves: 6–8
Preparation: 1 hour + 14–18 hours 30 minutes to rise
Cooking: 25 minutes
Level: 3

OLIVE LADDER BREAD

Combine the yeast and ½ cup (125 ml) of water in a small bowl and set aside until frothy, 5–10 minutes. • Add the remaining water and 2 cups (300 g) of bread flour and mix with a wooden spoon until the mixture resembles a thick batter. Cover with plastic wrap (cling film) and let rest for 2–3 hours at room temperature. • Add the remaining 2 cups (300 g) bread flour, whole-wheat flour, buckwheat flour, salt, oil, and olives and mix to form a soft dough. • Turn out onto a floured work surface and knead until smooth and elastic, about 10 minutes. Add a little extra bread flour if the dough is too sticky. Place the dough in an oiled bowl and let rise for 1 hour. • Divide the dough into four equal portions. Working with one piece at a time, flatten the dough into a 12 x 4-inch (30 x 10-cm) rectangle about ½ inch (1 cm) thick. Use a sharp knife to make four deep cuts across the dough in each loaf. Begin the

2	(¼-ounce/7-g) packages active dry yeast or 1 ounce (25 g) fresh compressed yeast
3	cups (750 ml) warm water
4	cups (600 g) bread flour + more if
2	cups (300 g) whole-wheat (wholemeal) flour
¼	cup (30 g) buckwheat flour
2	teaspoons salt
2	tablespoons extra-virgin olive oil
2	cups (300 g) black olives, chopped
	Extra-virgin olive oil
	Sea salt, to sprinkle

Serves: 12–16
Preparation: 1 hour + 3–4 hours and 30 minutes to rise
Cooking: 20–25 minutes
Level: 3

cuts $\frac{1}{2}$-inch (1-cm) in from the edge to create a border around the loaf. When you have made four cuts, gently pull the top and bottom of the dough to stretch the cuts, making them look like rungs on a ladder. Repeat with the remaining pieces of dough. • Transfer the loaves to oiled baking sheets and let rise for 30 minutes at room temperature. • Preheat the oven to 400°F (200°C/gas 6). • Brush each loaf with oil and sprinkle with a little sea salt. • Bake for 20–25 minutes until the loaves are risen and golden brown. • Cool on wire racks.

See photograph on the following page

FRENCH BAGUETTES

Combine the yeast, sugar, and $1/2$ cup (125 ml) of water in a small bowl and set aside until frothy, 5–10 minutes. • Combine 4 cups (600 g) of the flour and the salt in a large bowl and add the yeast mixture and remaining water. Stir well, adding enough extra flour to make a soft but kneadable dough. • Turn out onto a floured work surface and knead until smooth and elastic, about 10 minutes. • Place in oiled bowl and let rise until doubled in bulk, about 2 hours. • Divide the dough into three equal portions. Roll each piece out into an oval shape and roll up tightly, jelly-roll fashion. Roll the shaped dough back and forth to lengthen the baguette.
• Brush with the beaten egg white and dust with flour. Using a very sharp knife, slash the tops of the baguettes diagonally at 4-inch (10-cm) intervals. • Let rise until doubled in bulk, about 30 minutes.
• Preheat the oven to 425°F (220°C/gas 7).
• Bake for 20–30 minutes, until golden.

2   ($1/4$-ounce/7-g) packages active dry yeast or 1 ounce (25 g) fresh compressed yeast
1   tablespoon sugar
2   cups (500 ml) warm water
5   cups (750 g) bread flour
2   teaspoons salt
1   large egg white, beaten, to glaze

Serves: 12–16
Preparation: 30 minutes
   + 2 hours 30 minutes
   to rise
Cooking: 20–30 minutes
Level: 2

THYME AND OLIVE BREAD

Starter: Mix the flour and salt in a large bowl. • Place the water and yeast in another bowl and stir until the yeast is dissolved. Stir the yeast mixture into the flour mixture. Leave to rise for 8 hours (or overnight) in a warm place.

Dough: Put 3 cups (450 g) of the flour in a large bowl. Make a well in the center and add the starter, olives, thyme, salt, and pepper. Mix until the flour is incorporated and you have a thick dough. • Tip the dough out onto a floured work surface and knead until smooth and elastic, about 10 minutes. • Divide the dough into two equal portions and shape each one into an oval loaf. Let rise until doubled in bulk, about 1 hour. • Preheat the oven to 400°F (200°C/gas 6).

• Spray the loaves with water and place in the oven. Spray with water every 10 minutes during baking. Bake for 45–55, until risen and golden brown.

• Let cool on a wire rack.

Starter

2 cups (300 g) bread flour
1/2 teaspoon salt
2 cups (500 ml) lukewarm water
2 teaspoons active dry yeast

Dough

4 cups (600 g) bread flour
1 cup (100 g) large black olives, pitted and chopped
1 tablespoon finely chopped fresh thyme
1 teaspoon salt
1 teaspoon freshly ground black pepper

Serves: 12
Preparation: 30 minutes + 9 hours to rise
Cooking: 45–55 minutes
Level: 3

GRISSINI (BREAD STICKS)

Combine the yeast, malt syrup, oil, and 1/2 cup (125 ml) of water in a small bowl. Set aside until frothy, 5–10 minutes.
• Combine the flour and salt in a large bowl. Add the yeast mixture and enough of the remaining water to make a soft dough. • Turn out onto a floured work surface and knead until smooth and elastic, about 10 minutes. • Shape the dough into a ball, lightly brush with oil, and let rise until doubled in bulk, about 1 hour. • Divide the dough into four equal portions, Cut each one into strips about 1/2 inch (1 cm) thick. Shape by holding the ends and pulling gently until about 8 inches (20 cm) long. Alternatively, divide the dough into 20 small pieces and roll each into a rope about 12 inches (30 cm) long. • Roll in the sesame or poppy seeds. Place on oiled baking sheets.
• Preheat the oven to 425°F (220°C/gas 7). Bake for 20 minutes until crisp and golden brown. Cool on a wire rack.

1 (1/4-ounce/7-g) package active dry yeast or 1/2 ounce (15 g) fresh compressed yeast
1 tablespoon malt syrup or honey
2 tablespoons extra-virgin olive oil
11/4 cups (300 ml) warm water
31/4 cups (500 g) bread flour
1 teaspoon salt
1/2 cup (70 g) sesame seeds or poppy seeds

Serves: 6–8
Preparation: 25 minutes + 1 hour to rise
Cooking: 20 minutes
Level: 3

MUSHROOM CIABATTA

Soak the porcini in the water for 1 hour. Drain, reserving the liquid. Strain the liquid, then measure out 1½ cups (325 ml). Chop the porcini. • Heat 1 tablespoon of oil over medium heat and sauté the fresh mushrooms and garlic until soft. Simmer to reduce the mushroom liquid. Add the porcini then set aside. • Warm the porcini liquid. Combine in a bowl with the yeast. Set aside until frothy, 5–10 minutes. • Mix the flour and salt in a bowl. Add the yeast and half the mushroom mixture. Mix well, then knead until smooth and elastic. Put in an oiled bowl and let rise until doubled in bulk, about 2 hours. • Divide the dough in half. Shape into large flat ovals. Spread with the re-maining mushrooms then roll up, jelly-roll style, tucking in the ends. Flatten the loaves then roll up again and shape into ovals.

• Place on a baking sheet sprinkled with cornmeal. Cover with a damp cloth and let rise until doubled in bulk, about 2 hours.

• Preheat the oven to 400°F (200°C/gas 6).

• Bake for 40 minutes until golden.

1	ounce (30 g) dried porcini mushrooms
1¾	cups (430 ml) warm water
2	tablespoons extra-virgin olive oil
8	ounces (250 g) fresh mushrooms, sliced
2	cloves garlic, finely chopped
1	(¼-ounce/7-g) package active dry yeast or ½ ounce (15 g) fresh compressed yeast
4	cups (600 g) bread flour
1	teaspoon salt
	Cornmeal, to sprinkle

Serves: 12–16
Preparation: 30 minutes
   + 1 hour to soak
   + 4 hours to rise
Cooking: 50 minutes
Level: 3

FRENCH GOAT CHEESE AND HERB ROLLS

Combine the yeast and water in a small bowl and set aside until frothy, 5–10 minutes. • Mix the flour, salt, and pepper in a large bowl. • Whisk together the oil and warm milk in a small bowl. • Add the milk and yeast mixtures to the bowl with the flour and mix with a wooden spoon until the ingredients combine to form a shaggy ball. • Turn the dough out onto a floured work surface and begin to knead, adding flour as necessary to keep the dough from sticking. Continue kneading until the dough is smooth and elastic, about 10 minutes. Flatten the dough out and dot the surface with small pieces of goat cheese. • Roll up the dough, enclosing the cheese. Knead very briefly to soften and distribute the cheese (there should still be some visible pieces). • Place the dough in an oiled bowl and let rise until doubled in bulk,

2	(1/4-ounce/7-g) packages active dry yeast or 1 ounce (25 g) fresh compressed yeast
1/3	cup (90 ml) warm water
5	cups (750 g) bread flour + extra, as needed
2	teaspoons salt
1	teaspoon freshly ground black pepper
2	tablespoons extra-virgin olive oil
2/3	cup (180 ml) warm milk
8	ounces (250 g) chèvre or other fresh goat cheese, cut in small cubes or crumbled
2	tablespoons finely chopped fresh parsley
2	tablespoons finely chopped fresh basil
2	tablespoons finely chopped fresh dill
1	large egg, beaten, to brush

Serves: 12–14
Preparation: 25 minutes
  + 4 hours to rise
Cooking: 20 minutes
Level: 2

about 3 hours. • Roll the dough out into a rectangle measuring about 12 x 15 inches (30 x 40 cm). Sprinkle with the herbs, then roll it up, jelly-roll style.
• Use a sharp knife to cut the roll into 1-inch (2.5-cm) thick slices. • Oil two baking sheets and place the slices on the sheets, spacing well. Brush with half the beaten egg. • Let the rolls rise until doubled in bulk, about 1 hour. • Preheat the oven to 400°F (200°C/gas 6).
• Brush the rolls with the remaining beaten egg. • Bake for 20 minutes or until risen and golden. • Let cool on a wire rack.

See photograph on the following page

BASIL AND RED BELL PEPPER PUGLIESE

Combine the yeast, $^1/_2$ cup (125 ml) of water, and sugar in a small bowl and set aside until frothy, 5–10 minutes. • Combine the flour and salt in a large bowl. Add the basil, bell pepper, oil, yeast mixture, and enough of the remaining water to make a kneadable dough. • Turn the dough out onto a floured work surface and knead until smooth and elastic, about 10 minutes. • Place the dough in an oiled bowl and cover with plastic wrap (cling film). Let rise until doubled in bulk, about 2 hours. • Preheat the oven to 425°F (220°C/gas 7) • Place the dough on an oiled baking sheet. Push down the sides of the loaf and tuck them under the dough. Repeat twice. This will create a tight surface over the loaf. • Brush with water and let rise until doubled in bulk, about 1 hour. • Brush with water again and dust with flour. • Bake for 45 minutes until the loaf sounds hollow when tapped on the bottom. • Let cool on a wire rack.

2   ($^1/_4$-ounce/7-g) packages active dry yeast or 1 ounce (25 g) fresh compressed yeast

2   cups (500 ml) warm water

$^1/_2$ teaspoon sugar

5   cups (750 g) bread flour

1   teaspoon salt

Small bunch fresh basil, finely chopped

5   ounces (150 g) roasted bell pepper (capsicum) pieces in oil, drained and chopped

$^1/_2$ cup (125 ml) extra-virgin olive oil

Serves: 10–12
Preparation: 40 minutes
 + 3 hours to rise
Cooking: 45 minutes
Level: 3

ROSEMARY, LEMON, AND PINE NUT LOAF

Preheat oven to 375°F (190°C/gas 5).
• Lightly brush or spray a 9 x 5 inch
(12 x 22 cm) loaf pan with olive oil and
dust with flour. • Place the lemon zest,
rosemary, and pine nuts in a bowl. Mix to
combine. • Combine the flour, baking
powder, parsnip, and Parmesan in a
separate bowl. Make a well in the center
of the flour mixture. • Beat the
buttermilk, oil, and lemon juice to
combine in a small bowl. Pour into the
flour mixture. Mix quickly and lightly to
form a soft dough. • Press half the
mixture into the prepared pan. Sprinkle
with half the pine nut mixture. Top with
the remaining dough. Mix the remaining
pine nut mixture with the extra flour.
Sprinkle over the surface of loaf. • Bake
for 40–45 minutes or until risen and
golden brown. • Serve warm or at
room temperature.

2	tablespoons finely grated lemon zest
2	tablespoons fresh rosemary
2	tablespoons pine nuts
2	cups (300 g) all-purpose (plain) flour + 1 tablespoon extra
2	teaspoons baking powder
1	cup (150 g) grated parsnip or potato
1	tablespoon freshly grated Parmesan
1	cup (250 ml) buttermilk
1	tablespoon extra-virgin olive oil
2	tablespoons freshly squeezed lemon juice

Serves: 8–10
Preparation: 25 minutes
Cooking: 40–45 minutes
Level: 2

OLIVE LOAF

Preheat the oven to 350°F (180°C/gas 4). • Butter a 9 x 5-inch (13 x 23-cm) loaf pan. • Combine the flour and baking powder in a large bowl. Make a well in the center and add the eggs, one at a time, stirring until just blended after each addition. Add the wine and oil and stir until smooth. • Stir in the ham, salt pork, olives, and cheese. Season with salt and pepper. • Pour the batter into the prepared pan. • Bake for about 1 hour, until a toothpick inserted into the center comes out clean. • Cool the loaf in the pan for 15 minutes. • Serve warm or at room temperature.

- 1²/₃ cups (250 g) all-purpose (plain) flour
- 1 teaspoon baking powder
- 4 large eggs
- ¹/₂ cup (125 ml) dry white wine
- ¹/₂ cup (125 ml) extra-virgin olive oil
- 8 ounces (250 g) ham, diced
- 5 ounces (150 g) salt pork or lardons (fat bacon), diced
- 1¹/₂ cups (150 g) thinly sliced pitted black olives
- 1¹/₄ cups (150 g) freshly grated Parmesan cheese
- Salt and freshly ground black pepper

Serves: 4
Preparation: 15 minutes
Cooking: 1 hour
Level: 1

SOUPS

MINESTRONE

Heat the oil in a large, deep saucepan over medium heat. Add the onion and garlic and sauté until softened, about 5 minutes. • Add the potatoes and sauté for 5 minutes. • Add the carrots, celery, and zucchini and sauté for 5 minutes. • Pour in the beef stock and tomatoes. Add the Parmesan crust. • Bring to a boil and simmer, covered, for 1 hour. If the soup becomes too thick, add more stock. • Add the parsley and cannellini beans and simmer for 10 minutes. • Discard the Parmesan crust. • Season the soup with salt and pepper. • Serve hot.

$1/3$	cup (90 ml) extra-virgin olive oil
1	medium onion, thinly sliced
1	clove garlic, finely chopped
3	medium potatoes, peeled and diced
3	carrots, thinly sliced
4	stalks celery, thinly sliced
4	zucchini (courgettes), thinly sliced
4	cups (1 liter) beef stock (see Easy French Onion Soup, page 150)
$1^{2}/3$	cups (400 g) chopped tomatoes or 1 (14-ounce/400-g) can, with juice
	Piece of Parmesan cheese rind
1	tablespoon finely chopped parsley
1	(14-ounce/400-g) can cannellini beans, drained
	Salt and freshly ground black pepper

Serves: 4–6
Preparation: 15 minutes
Cooking: 1 hour 25 minutes
Level: 1

■■■ *The Parmesan rind imparts a lovely flavor to this classic Italian soup. However, if you can't get it, don't worry—the soup will still be delicious without it.*

GAZPACHO

Soak the bread in a little water until softened, squeezing out the excess moisture. (The bread helps to thicken the soup and give it a nice consistency). • Process the tomatoes, cucumber, bell pepper, onion, and garlic in a food processor. • Strain through a sieve into a bowl and set aside. • Clean the bowl of the food processor. • Process the bread, oil, and vinegar until well blended. • Mix in the cumin and season with salt. • Add a little water and mix into the soup. • Add a few ice cubes and chill. Add more water if needed. • Serve chilled, with the cucumber on top.

2 slices day-old bread
4 pounds (2 kg) tomatoes, coarsely chopped
1 cucumber, peeled and diced
1 green bell pepper (capsicum), seeded and diced
1 small onion, peeled and diced
2 cloves garlic, finely chopped
5 tablespoons extra-virgin olive oil
1–2 tablespoons good-quality wine vinegar
1 teaspoon ground cumin
Salt
1/2 cup (125 ml) chilled water + extra, as needed
Ice cubes, to serve
1/2 cucumber, diced, to garnish

■■■Gazpacho is a chilled Spanish soup made from raw tomatoes and other vegetables. Packed with vitamins and very refreshing, it is perfect for hot summer days. There are many versions; this is a classic one, just as it is made where it originates in Andalucía, southern Spain.

Serves: 6–8
Preparation: 15 minutes + time to chill
Level: 1

FISH, TOMATO, AND GARBANZO BEAN SOUP

Sauté the onion in the oil in a large, deep saucepan over medium heat until the onion has softened, about 3 minutes.
• Add the coriander, cumin, and chile. Sauté until aromatic, 2 minutes. • Stir in the tomatoes, garbanzo beans, and fish stock and bring to a boil. • Decrease the heat and simmer, uncovered, for 15 minutes. • Add the fish and cook until the fish begins to flake, about 5 minutes.
• Remove from the heat and add the couscous. • Cover and let stand until the couscous is tender and puffed, about 10 minutes. • Serve hot with a dollop of yogurt and a sprinkling of parsley and mint.

1 onion, finely chopped

1 tablespoon extra-virgin olive oil

1 teaspoon ground coriander

1 teaspoon ground cumin

1 green chile, finely sliced

1²/3 cups (400 g) chopped tomatoes

1 (14-ounce/400-g) can garbanzo beans (chickpeas), drained

4 cups (1 liter) fish stock (see page 243)

1 pound (500 g) firm-textured white fish, cut into large pieces

1/3 cup (70 g) couscous

Plain yogurt, to serve

Finely chopped fresh parsley, to garnish

Fresh mint leaves, to garnish

Serves: 4–6
Preparation: 10 minutes
  + 10 minutes to stand
Cooking: 25 minutes
Level: 1

EASY FRENCH ONION SOUP

Beef Stock: Place all the ingredients in a large saucepan and simmer over low heat for 3 hours. Skim off the scum. Let the stock cool then strain through a fine metal sieve.

Soup: Melt the butter in a large saucepan over low heat. • Add the onions and garlic. Cover and simmer, stirring often, until the onions are golden, 30–35 minutes. • Stir in the flour and cook, stirring constantly, for 2 minutes. • Gradually pour in the stock, stirring constantly, and bring to a boil. Decrease the heat, cover, and simmer for 30 minutes. • Season with salt and pepper. • Preheat the broiler (grill). • Toast one side of the bread. Turn over and top the uncooked side with Gruyère. Broil until golden. • Ladle the soup into bowls and arrange a cheese toast on top. • Serve hot.

■■■ *This soup is best made with homemade beef stock. Beef stock is not difficult to make but it does take several hours to cook. The recipe given here will make about 3 quarts (3 liters) of stock, considerably more than is required for this soup. Freeze the extra stock and use it for other soups or risottos in this book.*

Beef Stock
1 onion, quartered
1 carrot, halved
1 leek
2 stalks celery
2 bay leaves
   Small bunch parsley
2 cloves garlic
2 ripe tomatoes
1 tablespoon sea salt
3 pounds (1.5 kg) stew or boiling beef
2 pounds (1 kg) beef bones
5 quarts (5 liters) water

Soup
$1/4$ cup (60 g) butter
$1^1/2$ pounds (750 g) onions, thinly sliced
1 clove garlic, sliced
2 teaspoons flour
5 cups (1.25 liters) beef stock
   Salt and freshly ground black pepper
4 slices French bread,
$1/2$ cup (60 g) freshly grated Gruyère

Serves: 4
Preparation: 30 minutes
Cooking: 4 hours
Level: 2

ROASTED TOMATO AND BELL PEPPER SOUP

Preheat the oven to 425°F (220°C/gas 7). • Oil a large baking dish. • Put the tomatoes and bell peppers in the prepared dish in a single layer. Roast until the skins are blistered, about 20 minutes. • Let cool. • Remove and discard the skins from the tomatoes and bell peppers, then coarsely chop. • Sauté the onions and garlic in the oil in a large, deep saucepan over low heat until the onion has softened, about 5 minutes. • Add the cumin and coriander and cook until aromatic, 1–2 minutes. • Add the tomatoes, bell peppers, and chicken stock. Bring to a boil. • Decrease the heat and simmer for 30 minutes. • Stir in the bread and balsamic vinegar. Season with salt and pepper. • Simmer for 10 minutes. • Serve hot, sprinkled with the Parmesan.

2 pounds (1 kg) tomatoes

2 red bell peppers (capsicums)

2 onions, finely chopped

3 cloves garlic, finely chopped

3 tablespoons extra-virgin olive oil

2 teaspoons ground cumin

1 teaspoon ground coriander

4 cups (1 liter) chicken stock (see Leek and Potato Soup, page 158)

2 slices white bread, crusts removed and crumbled

1 tablespoon balsamic vinegar

Salt and freshly ground black pepper

1/2 cup (60 g) freshly grated Parmesan

Serves: 4–6
Preparation: 30 minutes
Cooking: 65 minutes
Level: 2

EGG AND LEMON SOUP WITH MEATBALLS

Meatballs: Mix the beef, onion, parsley, rice, and egg in a large bowl with your hands. • Season well with salt and pepper. • Shape the mixture into small balls and roll in the cornstarch.

Soup: Bring the beef stock to a boil with the butter. • Decrease the heat and add the meatballs to the stock. • Cover and simmer for 45 minutes. • Let cool slightly. • Beat the egg and lemon juice together in a medium bowl. • Add a scant 1/2 cup (100 ml) of warm stock to the egg mixture. • Pour this mixture back into the stock and heat over low heat. • Season with salt and pepper. • Sprinkle with the parsley and serve hot.

Meatballs

1 pound (500 g) ground (minced) beef

1 medium onion, finely chopped

2 tablespoons finely chopped fresh parsley

1/2 cup (50 g) cooked short-grain rice

1 large egg, beaten

Salt and freshly ground black pepper

1/3 cup (50 g) cornstarch (cornflour

Soup

4 cups (1 liter) beef stock (see Easy French Onion Soup, page 150)

1/4 cup (60 g) butter

1 large egg

1/3 cup (90 ml) freshly squeezed lemon juice

1 tablespoon finely chopped fresh parsley

Serves: 4–6
Preparation: 15 minutes
Cooking: 1 hour
Level: 2

ITALIAN GARLIC AND BEAN SOUP

Sauté the onion and garlic in the butter in a large, deep saucepan over medium heat until the onion has softened, about 5 minutes. • Add the pancetta. Sauté for 3 minutes. • Add the celery and sauté for 2 minutes • Add the chicken stock, tomatoes, zucchini, thyme, and bay leaves. Simmer for 15 minutes. • Add the beans and simmer for 10 minutes. • Season with salt and pepper and serve hot.

1	onion, finely diced
8	cloves garlic, thinly sliced
2	tablespoons butter
1²/₃ cups (200 g)	diced pancetta
2	stalks celery, diced
8	cups (2 liters) chicken stock (see Leek and Potato Soup, page 158)
3	tomatoes, peeled, seeded, and diced
2	zucchini (courgettes), diced
8	sprigs fresh thyme, leaves only
2	bay leaves
1	(14-ounce/400-g) can cannellini beans, drained
1	(14-ounce/400-g) can borlotti or pinto beans, drained
	Salt and freshly ground black pepper

■■■*If you like garlic, this is the soup for you! If liked, increase the amount of garlic to 12–15 cloves. Garlic is very good for you and is believed to lower blood pressure and cholesterol and help prevent cancer and atherosclerosis. It also tastes great and stimulates the appetite.*

Serves: 6–8
Preparation: 15 minutes
Cooking: 35 minutes
Level: 1

LEEK AND POTATO SOUP

Chicken Stock: Put the chicken in a large stock pot. Pour in the water and bring to a gentle simmer over medium heat. • Skim off any scum that forms on the surface. • Add the onions, carrots, celery, parsley, bay leaves, and salt and return to a gentle simmer. • Reduce the heat and simmer for 3–4 hours, adding boiling water as needed to keep the chicken covered. • Turn off the heat and remove the chicken and vegetables. Let the stock cool then strain through a fine metal sieve. • Refrigerate until the fat hardens on the top. Discard the fat.

Soup: Sauté the pancetta in the butter in a large, deep saucepan over medium heat for 5 minutes. • Add the onion and sauté for 5 minutes. • Add the potatoes and sauté for 5 minutes. • Add the stock, leek, and bay leaf and bring to a boil. • Decrease the heat and simmer until the potatoes are cooked, 15–20 minutes. • Add the cream and nutmeg and season with salt and pepper. • Stir in the Parmesan and serve hot.

Chicken Stock

1	(3-pound/1.5-kg) chicken
5	quarts (5 liters) water
2	onions, quartered
2	carrots, halved
1	stalk celery
	Small bunch parsley
2	bay leaves
	Salt and freshly ground black pepper

Soup

5	ounces (150 g) pancetta, chopped
2	tablespoons butter
1	onion, finely chopped
1	pound (500 g) potatoes, peeled and diced
3	cups (750 ml) chicken stock
1	large leek, sliced
1	bay leaf
1/3	cup (90 ml) light (single) cream
1	teaspoon nutmeg
1/2	cup (60 g) freshly grated Parmesan

Serves: 4–6
Preparation: 20 minutes
Cooking: 30–35 minutes
Level: 1

SWEET POTATO AND ROSEMARY SOUP

Sauté the onion, garlic, and rosemary in the oil in a large, deep saucepan over medium heat until the onion has softened, about 5 minutes. • Add the sun-dried tomato pesto and sauté for 1 minute. • Add the carrot, potato, and sweet potato and sauté for 5 minutes. • Add the chicken stock and season with salt and pepper. Bring to a boil. • Decrease the heat and simmer until the vegetables are tender, 30–40 minutes. • Purée the soup in a food processor. • Return to the pan and heat through before serving. Add more stock if the soup is too thick. • Serve hot, drizzled with the oil.

■■■*Sun-dried tomato pesto is available commercially but can also be made easily at home. Soak 1 cup (125 g) of sun-dried tomatoes in warm water until softened, about 10 minutes. Combine in a food processor with 2 tablespoons each of chopped fresh basil and parsley, 4 cloves garlic, 2 tablespoons balsamic vinegar, 1 tablespoon tomato paste, 2 peeled tomatoes, $^1/_2$ cup (125 ml) extra-virgin olive oil, $^1/_2$ cup (60 g) grated Parmesan, salt, and pepper. Blend until smooth.*

1 **medium onion, finely chopped**

2 **cloves garlic, finely chopped**

1 **tablespoon finely chopped fresh rosemary**

3 **tablespoons extra-virgin olive oil**

2 **tablespoons sun-dried tomato pesto**

1 **medium carrot, diced**

1 **large potato, diced**

1$^1/_2$ **pounds (750 g) sweet potatoes, diced**

4 **cups (1 liter) chicken stock (see Leek and Potato Soup, page 158) + more as needed**

Salt and freshly ground black pepper

Rosemary-infused olive oil, to serve

Serves: 4–6
Preparation: 25 minutes
Cooking: 1 hour
Level: 1

ALMOND SOUP

Heat 1/4 cup (60 ml) of oil in a large frying pan over medium heat. Add the almonds, garlic, parsley, and 4 slices of bread and sauté until the garlic turns pale gold, about 3 minutes. • Combine in a food processor with the cumin, saffron, and a little chicken stock and process until smooth. • Transfer to a large, deep saucepan and pour in the remaining chicken stock and milk. Season with salt and pepper. • Bring to a boil over medium heat. Decrease the heat to low and simmer for 15 minutes. • Meanwhile, sauté the remaining bread in the remaining 2 tablespoons of oil until crisp. • Return the soup to a boil. • Cover, remove from the heat, and let stand for 5 minutes. • Serve hot, topped with the croutons.

1/4 cup (60 ml) + 2 tablespoons extra-virgin olive oil

1 1/4 cups (200 g) almonds

1 clove garlic

1 tablespoon finely chopped fresh parsley

8 slices day-old whole-wheat (wholemeal) bread, cut in squares

1 teaspoon ground cumin

1/2 teaspoon ground saffron

4 cups (1 liter) chicken stock (see Leek and Potato Soup, page 158)

1 cup (250 ml) milk

Salt and freshly ground black pepper

Serves: 4
Preparation: 20 minutes
Cooking: 35 minutes
Level: 1

SPANISH SPLIT PEA SOUP

Sauté the paprika, onions, and garlic in the oil in a large, deep saucepan over medium heat until aromatic and the onions have softened, about 5 minutes. • Add the bell pepper, carrot, and potatoes. Toss the vegetables thoroughly in the onion mixture. Simmer for 10 minutes, stirring constantly. • Add the water, split peas, and stock. Season with salt and pepper. • Simmer, uncovered, until the peas are very tender, about 30 minutes. • Cut the kernels from the corn. Reserve $1/2$ cup (60 g) of corn. Add the remainder to the soup and simmer for 2 minutes. • Process the soup in a blender or food processor until thick and smooth. • Serve hot, garnished with the reserved corn, parsley, and yogurt.

1 tablespoon sweet paprika

2 onions, finely chopped

1 clove garlic, finely chopped

1 tablespoon extra-virgin olive oil

1 green bell pepper (capsicum), finely chopped

1 carrot, thinly sliced

3 medium potatoes, peeled and diced

2 cups (200 g) dried green split peas

3 cups (750 ml) water

8 cups (2 liters) chicken stock (see Leek and Potato Soup, page 158) or vegetable stock (see page 251)

Salt and freshly ground black pepper

2 ears (cobs) fresh corn

Fresh parsley to garnish

Plain yogurt to serve

Serves: 4–6
Preparation: 30 minutes
Cooking: 45 minutes
Level: 2

ROASTED EGGPLANT AND BELL PEPPER SOUP

Broil (grill) the eggplants and bell peppers until the skins are blackened all over. • Wrap them in a paper bag for 10 minutes, then remove the skins and seeds (from the bell peppers). • Chop the eggplant and bell peppers coarsely and set aside. • Sauté the garlic and tomatoes in the oil in a large, deep saucepan over medium heat for 2 minutes. • Add the eggplant, bell peppers, and vegetable stock. Season with salt and pepper. • Simmer for 4 minutes. Remove from the heat and let cool slightly. • Process the soup in a blender or food processor until smooth. • Return the soup to the pan. • Simmer until heated through, about 5 minutes. • Serve hot, garnished with the parsley and a drizzling of extra oil.

2   pounds (1 kg) eggplant (aubergines)

3   red bell peppers (capsicums)

2   cloves garlic, finely chopped

3   tomatoes, peeled and coarsely chopped

1   tablespoon extra-virgin olive oil + extra, to drizzle

2   cups (500 ml) vegetable stock (see page 251)

Salt and freshly ground black pepper

Fresh parsley leaves, to garnish

Serves: 4–6
Preparation: 30 minutes
Cooking: 30 minutes
Level: 2

VEGETABLE SOUP WITH PESTO

Combine the green beans, potatoes, carrots, zucchini, tomatoes, and onion in a large, deep saucepan with the water. Season with salt and pepper. • Bring to a boil and cook, stirring often, over low heat for 1 hour. • Add the pasta and cook until almost al dente. • Add the canned red and white kidney beans and return to a boil. • Serve hot, topping each serving with pesto.

4 ounces (125 g) green beans, cut into short lengths

3 medium potatoes, peeled and diced

3 medium carrots, diced

3 zucchini (courgettes), diced

3 tomatoes, finely chopped

1 medium onion, finely chopped

8 cups (2 liters) cold water

Salt and freshly ground black pepper

8 ounces (250 g) small soup pasta

1 cup (200 g) canned red kidney beans

1 cup (200 g) canned white kidney or cannellini beans

Pesto (see Vegetable Lasagna Stacks with Pesto, page 226)

Serves: 4–6
Preparation: 15 minutes
Cooking: 1 hour 15 minutes
Level: 1

■ ■ ■ *This fragrant soup is a summertime favorite in Provence, where it is known as* Soupe au pistou. *The basil sauce is almost identical to Italian pesto, which is hardly surprising since it originated just over the border in Liguria.*

BLACK KALE AND CORNMEAL SOUP

Sauté the onions and chilies in the oil in a large, deep saucepan over medium heat until the onions are softened, about 5 minutes. • Add the kale and sauté for 5 minutes. • Stir in the tomato paste and sauté for 5 minutes. • Pour in the water and mix well. Cover and simmer for 15 minutes. • Gradually sprinkle in the cornmeal, stirring constantly. • Cook, stirring almost constantly, until the cornmeal is well cooked, about 45 minutes. Add more boiling water during cooking if the soup becomes too thick. • Serve hot.

2 onions, finely chopped

2 fresh chiles, thinly sliced

Scant $1/2$ cup (100 ml) extra-virgin olive oil

2 bunches black kale, finely shredded

1 tablespoon tomato paste (concentrate)

6 cups (1.5 liters) boiling water + extra, as required

$1^2/3$ cups (250 g) finely ground yellow cornmeal

Serves: 4–6
Preparation: 10 minutes
Cooking: 1 hour 15 minutes
Level: 2

■ ■ ■ *This is a traditional Tuscan soup. Black kale, also known as Tuscan kale, dinosaur kale, lacinto kale, or cavolo nero in Italian, is now available in many farmers' markets. However, if you can't find it, substitute with the same quantity of curly kale or Swiss chard (silverbeet).*

NORTH AFRICAN FISH SOUP

Put the fish in a large bowl and drizzle with the lemon juice. Add half the saffron and sprinkle with salt. • Stir well and let marinate for 15 minutes. • Sauté the bell peppers in the oil in a large saucepan over medium heat until slightly softened, 8–10 minutes. • Transfer to a plate and set aside. • In the same pan, sauté the onions, garlic, tomatoes, celery, carrot, bay leaf, and orange zest for 5 minutes. • Pour in the water and bring to a boil. • Add the fish and simmer until cooked, 5–10 minutes. • Remove the fish from the pan and cover with a plate to keep warm. • Return the stock to a boil and add the bulgur. • Simmer until tender, 15–20 minutes. • Stir in the capers, remaining saffron, and cumin. • Put the fish in individual bowls and ladle the soup over the top. • Serve hot.

2	pounds (1 kg) mixed firm-textured fish, boned and diced
2	tablespoons freshly squeezed lemon juice
6	strands saffron, crumbled
1/2	teaspoon salt
3	red bell peppers (capsicums), seeded and cut into strips
1/4	cup (60 ml) extra-virgin olive oil
2	onions, chopped
4	cloves garlic, chopped
4	tomatoes, chopped
1	stalk celery, chopped
1	carrot, chopped
1	bay leaf
	Finely grated zest of 1 orange
8	cups (2 liters) water
1/4	cup (50 g) bulgur
20	capers
1/4	teaspoon cumin seeds

Serves: 6–8
Preparation: 45 minutes
Cooking: 35–45 minutes
Level: 1

CHUNKY POTATO SOUP WITH PANCETTA

Sauté the onion and pancetta in the butter in a large, deep saucepan over medium heat until browned, about 5 minutes. • Sprinkle with the paprika. Add the potatoes, ginger, marjoram, and bay leaf. Season with salt and pepper. Sprinkle with the flour and mix well. • Add the water and bring to a boil. • Simmer until the potatoes are tender, about 20 minutes. • Discard the bay leaf. Stir in the sour cream, parsley, garlic, and dill. • Simmer for 2 minutes over low heat. • Ladle into serving dishes and serve hot.

1 large onion, finely chopped

1/2 cup (60 g) diced pancetta

1/4 cup (60 g) butter

2 teaspoons sweet paprika

1 1/2 pounds (750 g) potatoes, peeled and diced

1 teaspoon ground ginger

2 teaspoons finely chopped fresh marjoram

1 bay leaf

Salt and freshly ground black pepper

2 tablespoons all-purpose (plain) flour

4 cups (1 liter) water

3/4 cup (200 ml) sour cream

2 tablespoons finely chopped fresh parsley

2 cloves garlic, finely chopped

2 teaspoons finely chopped fresh dill

Serves: 4
Preparation: 10 minutes
Cooking: 30 minutes
Level: 1

NORTH AFRICAN MUTTON SOUP

Combine the mutton, butter, onions, celery, half the parsley and cilantro, cinnamon, saffron, and ginger in a large, deep saucepan. Season with salt and pepper. Stir over medium heat until the butter has melted. • Pour in 1 quart (1 liter) of water. • Bring to a boil and simmer until reduced by half, 25–30 minutes. • Stir in the garbanzo beans and lentils. • Cook over low heat until the lentils are tender, about 2 hours. • Stir in the tomatoes, 2 quarts (2 liters) of water, and the remaining parsley and cilantro. • Bring to a boil. Decrease the heat and simmer for 10 minutes more. • Add the rice. • Mix the flour and 1/2 cup (125 ml) remaining water to a smooth paste in a small bowl. • Remove the soup from the heat and add the flour mixture, stirring constantly. • Return to the heat and cook for 15 minutes more, stirring constantly.

1	pound (500 g) mutton or lamb, diced
2	tablespoons clarified butter (ghee)
2	onions, finely chopped
1	stalk celery, finely chopped
1	tablespoon finely chopped fresh parsley
1	tablespoon finely chopped fresh cilantro (coriander)
1	stick cinnamon
4	strands saffron, crumbled
1/4	teaspoon ground ginger
	Salt and freshly ground black pepper
3	quarts (3 liters) cold water + 1/2 cup (125 ml)
1	cup (200 g) dried garbanzo beans (chickpeas), soaked overnight and drained

2 cups (250 g) brown lentils

2 pounds (1 kg) firm-ripe tomatoes, chopped

1/2 cup (100 g) short-grain rice

3 tablespoons all-purpose (plain) flour

2 tablespoons freshly squeezed lemon juice

Fresh cilantro (coriander) leaves, to garnish

Serves: 6–8
Preparation: 20 minutes + 12 hours to soak beans
Cooking: 3 hours
Level: 2

The soup should not be too thick. • Stir in the lemon juice. • Serve the soup hot, garnished with the cilantro.

■ ■ ■ This hearty dish falls somewhere between a soup and a stew. It makes a wonderful meal in itself. If you like spicy dishes, this soup is delicious with the addition of 1 to 2 thinly sliced fresh red chilies.

See photograph on the following page

MIDDLE EASTERN SOUP WITH BEEF, RICE, AND SPINACH

Sauté the onions, garlic, and carrot in 1/4 cup (60 ml) of oil in a large, deep saucepan over medium heat until lightly browned, about 5 minutes. • Add the beef and sauté until browned, about 10 minutes. • Pour in the water and tomatoes. Decrease the heat, cover, and simmer over low heat until the beef is tender, about 1 1/2 hours. • Stir in the rice and cook for 15 minutes. • Add the spinach and cinnamon. Season with salt and pepper. Simmer for 10 minutes more. • Add the parsley and remaining 2 tablespoons of oil just before serving.

2   onions, finely chopped

4   cloves garlic, finely chopped

1   small carrot, thinly sliced

1/4   cup (60 ml) + 2 tablespoons extra-virgin olive oil

1 1/2   pounds (750 g) stewing beef, diced

3   quarts (3 liters) cold water

2   tomatoes, finely chopped

3/4   cup (150 g) long-grain rice

1   pound (500 g) frozen spinach

1   teaspoon ground cinnamon

Salt and freshly ground black pepper

3   tablespoons finely chopped fresh parsley

Serves: 6–8
Preparation: 30 minutes
Cooking: 2 hours
   15 minutes
Level: 1

PASTA

PENNE WITH CHICKEN AND SPINACH

Cook the pasta in a large pot of salted, boiling water until al dente. • While the pasta is cooking, sauté the onion and garlic in the butter in a large frying pan over medium heat until softened, about 5 minutes. • Add the chicken and chicken stock. Simmer for 5 minutes. • Drain the pasta and add to the pan with the sauce. • Add the spinach and season with salt and pepper. Toss well. • Sprinkle with the pine nuts and serve at once.

■ ■ ■ *Use leftover roast or grilled chicken or prepare it especially for this recipe by lightly poaching a chicken breast in a little salted water or stock.*

1   **pound (500 g) penne**

1   **onion, finely chopped**

1   **clove garlic, finely chopped**

2   **tablespoons butter**

2   **cups (250 g) cooked chicken, shredded**

1/2 **cup (125 ml) chicken stock, hot (see Leek and Potato Soup, page 158)**

Small bunch baby spinach leaves, coarsely chopped

Salt and freshly ground black pepper

1/3 **cup (60 g) pine nuts, toasted**

Serves: 4–6
Preparation: 10 minutes
Cooking: 15 minutes
Level: 1

STORTELLI WITH ROASTED VEGETABLES

Preheat the oven to 400°F (200°C/ gas 6). • Blanch the tomatoes in a large pot of boiling water for 30 seconds. • Drain and let cool slightly. Peel and slice thickly. • Arrange the tomatoes, eggplant, zucchini, bell pepper, and onions in a single layer in a roasting pan. Season with salt and pepper and drizzle with 2 tablespoons of the oil. • Roast until the vegetables are tender and lightly browned, about 40 minutes. • Mix the remaining 3 tablespoons of oil, garlic, and basil in a small bowl. • Cook the pasta in a large pot of salted, boiling water until al dente. • Drain the pasta and put in a heated serving dish. Toss with the basil and oil mixture and roasted vegetables. • Serve hot, passing the Parmesan separately.

5	firm-ripe tomatoes
1	small eggplant (aubergine), thickly sliced
1	zucchini (courgette), thickly sliced
1	red or yellow bell pepper (capsicum), seeded and cut into quarters
2	onions, thickly sliced
	Salt and freshly ground black pepper
5	tablespoons extra-virgin olive oil
2	cloves garlic, finely chopped
24	fresh basil leaves, torn
1	pound (500 g) stortelli or fusilli
1/4	cup (30 g) freshly grated Parmesan, to serve

Serves: 4–6
Preparation: 20 minutes
Cooking: 50 minutes
Level: 1

FARFALLE WITH GOAT CHEESE AND ASPARAGUS

Sauté the onions and garlic in the butter and oil in a large frying pan over low heat until golden, 5–7 minutes. • Cook the pasta in a large pot of salted, boiling water for 5 minutes. • Add the asparagus and cook for 2 minutes. • Add the peas and cook for 2 minutes more. At this point the pasta should be al dente and the asparagus should be tender. • Drain and add to the pan with the onion and garlic mixture. Toss well. • Stir in the goat cheese and season generously with pepper. • Serve hot.

2	small red onions, thinly sliced
1	clove garlic, finely chopped
2	tablespoons butter
1	tablespoon extra-virgin olive oil
1	pound (500 g) farfalle
8	ounces (250 g) asparagus, trimmed and cut on the diagonal into short lengths
1	cup (150 g) frozen peas
8	ounces (250 g) chèvre or other fresh goat cheese, crumbled
	Freshly ground black pepper

Serves: 4–6
Preparation: 10 minutes
Cooking: 20 minutes
Level: 1

■ ■ ■ Farfalle *means "butterflies" in Italian, which is what this short pasta type resembles. In English the same pasta shape is called "bowties."*

CAVATELLI WITH PANCETTA, AND SUN-DRIED TOMATOES

Tomato Sauce: Sauté the onion in the oil in a large frying pan over medium heat until lightly browned, about 5 minutes. • Add the tomatoes and half the basil and season with salt. Simmer for 15–20 minutes over low heat. Stir in the remaining basil.

Pasta: Cook the pasta in a large pot of salted, boiling water until al dente. • Meanwhile, sauté the garlic and pancetta in the oil in a large frying pan over medium heat for 2 minutes until the garlic turns pale gold. • Drain the pasta and add to the pan with the pancetta.

• Stir in 2 cups of the tomato sauce, sun-dried tomatoes, and arugula. Season with salt and pepper. • Serve hot, topped with shavings of Parmesan cheese.

Tomato Sauce

1	onion, finely chopped
3	tablespoons extra-virgin olive oil
2	pounds (1 kg) tomatoes, peeled, or 2 (14-ounce/400-g) cans tomatoes, with juice
5	leaves fresh basil, torn

Pasta

1	pound (500 g) cavatelli or other short pasta
2	cloves garlic, finely chopped
3/4	cup (100 g) diced pancetta
1	tablespoon extra-virgin olive oil
1	cup (180 g) sun-dried tomatoes, chopped
1	bunch arugula (rocket)
	Salt and freshly ground black pepper
	Parmesan cheese, to serve

Serves: 4–6
Preparation: 15 minutes + time for sauce
Cooking: 25 minutes
Level: 1

■ ■ ■ *This is best with homemade tomato sauce but a well-seasoned store-bought sauce can be substituted.*

FARFALLE WITH SHRIMP AND ZUCCHINI

Remove the zucchini flowers and rinse carefully under cold running water.
• Slice the zucchini thinly lengthwise.
• Sauté the onion in the butter in a large frying pan over medium heat until softened, about 3 minutes. • Add the zucchini and season with salt and pepper. Cover and simmer over low heat for 10 minutes, stirring often. • Meanwhile, cook the pasta in a large pot of salted, boiling water until al dente.
• Add the shrimp and zucchini flowers to the pan with the sauce and simmer for 5 minutes. • Stir in the cream and simmer until heated through. • Drain the pasta and add to the pan with the sauce.
• Sprinkle with the parsley and toss well.
• Serve hot.

6 baby zucchini (courgettes), with flowers attached
1 onion, finely chopped
1/4 cup (60 g) butter
  Salt and freshly ground black pepper
1 pound (500 g) farfalle
1 pound (500 g) shrimp (prawn tails), peeled, and deveined
1/2 cup (125 ml) heavy (double) cream
2 tablespoons finely chopped fresh parsley

Serves: 4–6
Preparation: 15 minutes
Cooking: 20 minutes
Level: 1

■ ■ ■ *This is a traditional Italian recipe. Zucchini flowers are not always easy to find. If you can't find the baby zucchini with flowers attached, replace with four medium zucchini and skip the steps in the recipe regarding the flowers.*

PENNE WITH MELON

Cut the melons in half. Discard the seeds. • Remove the flesh; if you intend to serve the pasta in the melon shells, leave about 1/2 inch (1 cm) of flesh attached to the peel. • Chop the melon flesh coarsely and put in a large bowl. • Beat the oil, lemon zest, peppercorns, and salt in a small bowl and pour it over the chopped melon. • Cover with plastic wrap (cling film) and chill for 30 minutes. • Meanwhile, cook the pasta in a large pot of salted, boiling water until al dente. • Drain well. • Add the pasta to the melon mixture and toss well. • Spoon the mixture into the melon halves or serve in individual pasta bowls. Garnish with the pecorino. • Serve hot or at room temperature.

2   small cantaloupe (rock) melons

1/4   cup (60 ml) extra-virgin olive oil

    Finely grated zest of 1/2 lemon

1   teaspoon green peppercorns in brine

1/4   teaspoon salt

1   pound (500 g) penne rigate

3   ounces (100 g) aged pecorino cheese, in shavings

Serves: 4–6
Preparation: 25 minutes + 30 minutes to chill
Cooking: 10 minutes
Level: 1

■ ■ ■ *This dish will be only as good as the melon you use to make it. Choose in-season, locally grown melons at the height of summer for the perfect dish.*

SPAGHETTI WITH ORANGE

Cook the pasta in a large pot of salted, boiling water until al dente. • While the pasta is cooking, sauté the anchovies and garlic in the oil in a large frying pan over medium heat until the anchovies have dissolved and the garlic is pale gold, about 3 minutes. • Add the bread crumbs and simmer for 3 minutes. • Turn up the heat. Pour in the wine and let it evaporate. • Add the oranges and their juice. Simmer for 2 minutes. • Season with salt. • Drain the pasta and add to the pan with the sauce. Toss gently, sprinkle with the parsley, and serve hot.

1	pound (500 g) spaghetti
8	anchovy fillets, crumbled (optional)
2	cloves garlic, finely chopped
1/3	cup (90 ml) extra-virgin olive oil
3	tablespoons fine dry bread crumbs
1/4	cup (60 ml) dry white wine
4	oranges, peeled and cut into segments
	Salt
1	tablespoon finely chopped fresh parsley

Serves: 4–6
Preparation: 15 minutes
Cooking: 15 minutes
Level: 1

■ ■ ■ *For best results, use very fresh in-season oranges. Since oranges are in season during the winter months, this is a wonderful dish to brighten up long winter days and a good source of vitamin C just when you need it most.*

SPAGHETTI WITH SUN-DRIED TOMATOES

Cook the pasta in a large pot of salted, boiling water until al dente. • While the pasta is cooking, pour the oil from the sun-dried tomatoes—about ⅓ cup (90 ml)—into a large frying pan. • Heat over medium heat and add the tomatoes. Sauté for 1 minute and season with the red pepper and salt. Simmer over low heat until ready to serve. • Drain the pasta and add to the pan with the tomatoes. Sprinkle with the basil. Toss well. • Serve hot with the cheese.

1½ cups (250 g) sun-dried tomatoes in oil, finely sliced

Pinch of crushed red pepper flakes

Salt

1 pound (500 g) spaghetti

1 bunch fresh basil leaves, torn

3 ounces (90 g) caciocavallo or provolone cheese, shaved

Serves: 4
Preparation: 5 minutes
Cooking: 15 minutes
Level: 1

SPAGHETTI WITH SQUID

Bring a large saucepan of water to a boil. Use a slotted spoon or wire basket to carefully lower about a quarter of the squid into the water. • Cook until the squid turns white and becomes firm, 20–30 seconds. • Drain and plunge into iced water to stop the cooking process. Drain again. Set aside. • Repeat this process with all the squid. • Cook the pasta in a large pot of salted, boiling water until al dente. • Meanwhile, sauté the onion and garlic in the oil in a large frying pan over medium heat until softened, about 3 minutes. • Add the tomatoes, olives, fish stock, and wine. Bring to a boil. Simmer for 5 minutes. • Stir in the cilantro, mint, and squid. Season with salt and pepper. • Cook for 1–2 minutes until heated through. • Drain the pasta and add to the pan with the sauce. Toss well and serve hot.

1 pound (500 g) squid, cleaned and cut into rings
1 pound (500 g) spaghetti
1 onion, finely chopped
1 clove garlic, finely chopped
1 tablespoon extra-virgin olive oil
5 tomatoes, seeded and diced
1/2 cup (50 g) pitted kalamata olives, finely sliced
1/4 cup (60 ml) fish stock, hot (see page 243)
1/4 cup (60 ml) dry white wine
Small bunch of fresh cilantro (coriander) leaves
Small bunch of fresh mint leaves
Salt and freshly ground black pepper

Serves: 4–6
Preparation: 15 minutes
Cooking: 20 minutes
Level: 2

BUCATINI WITH BROCCOLI

Blanch the broccoli in a large pot of salted boiling water for 2 minutes. • Drain well and set aside. • Sauté the scallions in 2 tablespoons of the oil in a large frying pan over medium heat until softened, about 3 minutes. • Add the pine nuts and currants and simmer for 2 minutes. • Turn up the heat. Pour in the wine and simmer until it evaporates. • Add the broccoli and saffron water. Season with salt and pepper. • Cook for 10 minutes, using a wooden spoon to break up the broccoli. • Cook the pasta in a large pot of salted, boiling water until al dente. • Meanwhile, dissolve the anchovies in the remaining 1 tablespoon of oil in a separate small frying pan over medium heat, about 3 minutes. • Stir the anchovies into the broccoli sauce. • Drain the pasta and add to the pan with the sauce. Toss well. • Top with the shavings of Parmesan cheese and serve hot.

$1^{1}/_{2}$ pounds (750 g) broccoli, cut into small florets

6 scallions (spring onions), finely chopped

3 tablespoons extra-virgin olive oil

2 tablespoons pine nuts

2 tablespoons currants

1 cup (250 ml) dry white wine

1 teaspoon saffron dissolved in $^{1}/_{2}$ cup (125 ml) water

Salt and freshly ground black pepper

5 anchovy fillets, crumbled

1 pound (500 g) bucatini or spaghetti

2 ounces (60 g) Parmesan, shaved

Serves: 4–6
Preparation: 10 minutes
Cooking: 20 minutes
Level: 1

SPAGHETTI WITH MEATBALLS

Mix the beef, parsley, salami, Parmesan, 1 tablespoon of tomato paste, and egg in a large bowl. • Shape the mixture into balls about the size of golf balls. • Dry-fry the meatballs in a nonstick frying pan until cooked through, 10–15 minutes. Set aside. • Sauté the onion, basil, and oregano in the butter in a large saucepan over medium heat until the onion is softened, about 3 minutes. • Stir in the tomatoes, the remaining 2 tablespoons tomato paste, beef stock, wine, and sugar. • Cover and simmer for 30 minutes, stirring occasionally. • Cook the pasta in a large pot of salted, boiling water until al dente. • Drain and arrange on a serving plate. • Stir the meatballs into the tomato sauce and serve on top of the spaghetti.

1	pound (500 g) ground (minced) beef
2	tablespoons finely chopped fresh parsley
1/2	cup (60 g) diced salami
1/2	cup (60 g) freshly grated Parmesan
3	tablespoons tomato paste (concentrate)
1	large egg, lightly beaten
1	onion, chopped
1	tablespoon finely chopped fresh basil
1	teaspoon dried oregano
1	tablespoon butter
$1^{2}/_{3}$	cups (400 g) chopped tomatoes
1/2	cup (125 ml) beef stock (see Easy French Onion Soup, page 150)
1/2	cup (125 ml) dry white wine
1	teaspoon sugar
1	pound (500 g) spaghetti

Serves: 4–6
Preparation: 15 minutes
Cooking: 50 minutes
Level: 2

■ ■ ■ *If preferred, substitute the fresh tomatoes with 1 (14-ounce/400-g) can of tomatoes, with juice.*

TAGLIATELLE WITH SCALLOPS AND BREAD CRUMBS

Detach the corals from the scallops and set aside. • Fry the bread crumbs in 2 tablespoons of oil in a frying pan over medium heat until golden, about 3 minutes. Remove and set aside. • Sauté 2 tablespoons of parsley, the garlic, and red pepper in the remaining oil in the same frying pan over medium heat for 2 minutes. • Meanwhile, cook the pasta in a large pot of salted, boiling water until al dente. • Add the white parts of the scallops to the sauce. • Cook for 30 seconds until they start to turn opaque. Turn up the heat. Add the wine and the reserved scallop corals. Simmer for 30 seconds. • Drain the pasta and add to the pan with the sauce. • Toss gently. Sprinkle with the bread crumbs and the remaining 2 tablespoons of parsley. • Serve hot.

12 fresh sea scallops, preferably with their corals

1/2 cup (60 g) fine dry bread crumbs

1/2 cup (125 ml) extra-virgin olive oil

4 tablespoons finely chopped fresh parsley

2 cloves garlic, finely chopped

1 teaspoon crushed red pepper flakes

14 ounces (400 g) fresh tagliatelle

1/4 cup (60 ml) dry white wine

Serves: 4
Preparation: 10 minutes
Cooking: 15 minutes
Level: 2

TAGLIATELLE WITH MUSSELS

Soak the mussels in a large bowl of cold water for 1 hour. Drain well and scrub of any beards. • Place the mussels in a large pan, cover, and cook over medium-low heat until they are all open. Discard any that have not opened. Remove the mussels from their shells and set aside. • Blanch the tomatoes in a large pot of boiling water for 30 seconds. • Drain and let cool slightly. Peel, squeeze gently to remove the seeds, and chop coarsely. • Sauté the onion, garlic, celery, bell pepper, and mushrooms in the oil in a large frying pan over medium heat until softened, about 5 minutes. • Mix in the tomatoes, sun-dried tomatoes, wine, and tomato paste. Season with pepper. Bring to a boil. • Cover and simmer until the vegetables are tender, about 20 minutes. • Stir in the mussels. Simmer over medium heat for 5 minutes. • Cook the pasta in a large pot of salted, boiling water until al dente. • Drain and add to the sauce with the basil and toss gently. • Garnish with the basil. Serve hot.

2 pounds (1 kg) mussels, in shell

1¹/2 pounds (750 g) tomatoes

1 onion, chopped

2 cloves garlic, finely chopped

2 stalks celery, finely chopped

1 red bell pepper (capsicum), diced

4 ounces (125 g) mushrooms, diced

1 tablespoon extra-virgin olive oil

4 sun-dried tomatoes, finely chopped

¹/2 cup (125 ml) dry red wine

2 tablespoons tomato paste (concentrate)

Freshly ground black pepper

14 ounces (400 g) fresh tagliatelle

2 tablespoons finely chopped fresh basil + leaves to garnish

Serves: 4
Preparation: 15 minutes + 1 hour to soak
Cooking: 30 minutes
Level: 1

PAPPARDELLE CAPRESE

Mix the tomatoes, basil, mozzarella, capers, oil, and vinegar in a large bowl. • Cook the pasta in a large pot of salted, boiling water until al dente. • Drain well and add to the bowl with the tomato mixture. Toss gently. • Sprinkle with shavings of Parmesan and season with salt and pepper. • Serve hot.

6   **plum tomatoes, diced**

1   **bunch fresh basil leaves, coarsely chopped**

5   **ounces (150 g) fresh mozzarella cheese, diced**

1   **tablespoon salt-cured capers, rinsed**

2   **tablespoons extra-virgin olive oil**

1   **tablespoon balsamic or red wine vinegar**

14   **ounces (400 g) fresh pappardelle**

Shavings of fresh Parmesan cheese (optional)

Salt and freshly ground black pepper

Serves: 4
Preparation: 10 minutes
Cooking: 5 minutes
Level: 1

■ ■ ■ *This salad takes its name from the famous Italian salad—insalata caprese (see page 558 for our version), which is made with the finest-quality, fresh water buffalo-milk mozzarella, tomatoes, and basil.*

PAPPARDELLE WITH BOLOGNESE SAUCE

212

Sauté the pancetta, onion, carrot, celery, and garlic in the oil and butter in a large saucepan over medium heat until the vegetables have softened, about 5 minutes. • Add the beef and sauté until browned, about 5 minutes. • Turn up the heat. Pour in the wine and simmer until it evaporates. • Mix in the tomato paste and beef stock. Season with salt and pepper. Return to a boil. • Simmer over very low heat for 2–2$\frac{1}{2}$ hours, stirring occasionally. Add 2 tablespoons of milk whenever the sauce starts to dry out. • Cook the pasta in a large pot of salted, boiling water until al dente. • Drain and arrange on serving plates. • Spoon the sauce on top. • Sprinkle with the Parmesan and serve hot.

1   cup (125 g) diced unsmoked pancetta or bacon

1   small onion, finely chopped

1   small carrot, finely chopped

1   stalk celery, finely chopped

1   clove garlic, chopped

3   tablespoons extra-virgin olive oil

2   tablespoons butter

1   pound (500 g) ground (minced) beef

$\frac{1}{2}$ cup (125 ml) dry white wine

2   tablespoons tomato paste (concentrate)

$\frac{1}{2}$ cup (125 ml) beef stock (see Easy French Onion Soup, page 150)

Salt and freshly ground black pepper

$\frac{1}{2}$ cup (125 ml) milk

1   pound (500 g) fresh pappardelle

$\frac{1}{4}$ cup (30 g) freshly grated Parmesan

Serves: 4
Preparation: 20 minutes
Cooking: 3 hours
Level: 2

PASTA WITH BEANS

Place the beans in a large saucepan with the water, garlic, sage, and oil. Bring to a boil and simmer over low heat until tender, about 1$\frac{1}{2}$ hours. • Season with salt and drain, reserving the water.

Pasta Dough: Combine the flour and salt in a mound on a work surface and make a hollow in the center. • Break in the eggs and mix to make a smooth dough. • Knead until smooth and elastic, 15–20 minutes. • Shape into a ball, wrap in plastic wrap (cling film), and let rest for 30 minutes.

Sauce: Sauté the garlic and parsley in the oil in a saucepan over medium heat until pale gold, about 3 minutes. • Add the tomatoes and season with salt and pepper. Simmer for 20 minutes. • Add the beans and a few tablespoons of the cooking water. • Roll out the dough on a lightly floured surface into a thin sheet. Cut into irregularly shaped pieces. • Cook the pasta in a large pot of salted, boiling water until al dente. • Drain and serve with the sauce.

- 1 pound (500 g) dried red kidney or borlotti beans, soaked overnight
- 8 cups (2 liters) cold water
- 2 cloves garlic
- 1 bunch fresh sage
- 2 tablespoons extra-virgin olive oil
  Salt

Pasta Dough
- 2 cups (300 g) all-purpose (plain) flour
- $\frac{1}{4}$ teaspoon salt
- 3 large eggs

Sauce
- 2 cloves garlic, finely chopped
- 2 tablespoons finely chopped fresh parsley
- 2 tablespoons extra-virgin olive oil
- 6 tomatoes, diced
  Salt and freshly ground black pepper

Serves: 4–6
Preparation: 1 hour
  + 30 minutes to rest
  + 24 hours to soak
Cooking: 2 hours
Level: 2

FETTUCCINE WITH SALMON AND PEAS

Blanch the peas in a pot of boiling water for 2 minutes. • Drain well and set aside. • Bring the wine to a boil in a large frying pan. • Stir in 1 cup (250 ml) of cream and simmer until the sauce reduces and thickens, 3-4 minutes. • Meanwhile, cook the pasta in a large pot of salted, boiling water until al dente. • Chop four slices of the smoked salmon, scallions, and the remaining cream in a food processor. • Stir the salmon mixture into the sauce and simmer until heated through. • Cut the remaining salmon slices into strips. Add the salmon strips and peas to the sauce and season with pepper. • Drain the pasta and add to the pan with the sauce. Toss gently and serve hot.

1   cup (150 g) frozen peas

$1/4$ cup (60 ml) dry white wine

$1^{1}/4$ cups (300 ml) heavy (double) cream

14 ounces (400 g) fresh fettuccine

8   slices smoked salmon

3   scallions (spring onions), finely chopped

Freshly ground black pepper

Serves: 4
Preparation: 5 minutes
Cooking: 15 minutes
Level: 1

PIZZOCCHERI WITH POTATOES AND CABBAGE

Pasta Dough: Mound both flours and the salt on a surface and make a hollow in the center. • Mix in enough water to make a smooth dough. • Knead until smooth and elastic, 10–15 minutes. • Shape the dough into a ball, wrap in plastic wrap (cling film), and let rest for 30 minutes. • Roll out the dough on a lightly floured surface to ¼-inch (5-mm) thick. Cut into ½-inch (1-cm) strips, then into 2-inch (5-cm) rectangles. • Let rest until ready to cook.

Topping: Cook the potatoes and cabbage in a pot of salted, boiling water for 15 minutes. • Melt the butter in a small saucepan with the garlic, sage, and a pinch of salt. • Discard the garlic and sage. • Add the pasta to the potatoes and cabbage. Cook until the pasta is al dente and the vegetables are tender, 3–4 minutes. • Drain well. • Layer the pasta and vegetables in serving bowls with the Parmesan, Fontina, and melted butter. Season with pepper and serve hot.

Pasta Dough

2 cups (300 g) buckwheat flour

1 cup (150 g) all-purpose (plain) flour

Pinch of salt

¾ cup (180 ml) lukewarm water + extra, as needed

Topping

6 medium potatoes, peeled and cut into small chunks

½ head savoy or green cabbage, finely shredded

⅔ cup (150 g) butter

3 cloves garlic, lightly crushed but whole

1 sprig fresh sage

Salt and freshly ground black pepper

1 cup (125 g) freshly grated Parmesan

1¼ cups (150 g) freshly grated Fontina cheese

Serves: 4–6
Preparation: 1 hour + 30 minutes to rest
Cooking: 25 minutes
Level: 2

TORTELLINI WITH ONION CONFIT

Onion Confit: Sauté the onions in the butter in a medium saucepan over medium heat until softened, about 3 minutes. • Stir in the sugar and simmer for 2 minutes. • Add the thyme, wine, and vinegar. Simmer, stirring frequently, until the mixture reduces and thickens, about 40 minutes.

Tortellini: Pour the beef stock into a large saucepan and simmer until reduced by half. Keep warm. • Cook the pasta in a large pot of salted, boiling water until very al dente. • Drain and add to the pan with the stock. • Add the onion confit, peas, and parsley. Cook for about 2 minutes. • Serve hot.

Onion Confit

2   large onions, thinly sliced
2   tablespoons butter
2   teaspoons sugar
4   sprigs fresh thyme, leaves removed and stalks discarded
1   cup (250 ml) dry red wine
2   tablespoons red wine vinegar

Tortellini

1 1/2 cups (375 ml) beef stock (see Easy French Onion Soup, page 150)
1   pound (500 g) beef or veal-filled tortellini
1   cup (150 g) frozen peas
2   tablespoons finely chopped fresh parsley

Serves: 6–8
Preparation: 10 minutes
Cooking: 1 hour
Level: 1

SMOKED SALMON RAVIOLI WITH LEMON DILL SAUCE

Ravioli: Prepare the pasta dough. Combine the salmon, 1 tablespoon of egg white, cream, and dill in a food processor and process until well combined like a mousse. • Roll the dough out into a paper thin rectangle. Use a fluted 3-inch (7.5-cm) round cookie cutter to cut out rounds of pasta. • Place a teaspoon of mixture at the center of half the rounds of pasta. Top with the remaining pasta rounds. Press down with your fingertips to remove air and seal the edges. • Cook the pasta in a large pot of salted, boiling water until al dente, 2–3 minutes.

Lemon Dill Sauce: Melt the butter in a small saucepan. Add the flour and stir for 1 minute. • Turn up the heat. Add the wine, stirring until smooth, followed by the cream and lemon juice. Bring to a boil and simmer until the sauce has a pouring consistency. • Add the dill and season with salt and pepper. • Drain the pasta. Serve hot with the sauce.

Ravioli

4 ounces (125 g) smoked salmon

1 large egg white

1½ tablespoons light (single) cream

2 teaspoons coarsely chopped fresh dill

Pasta Dough (see Pasta with Beans, page 214)

1 teaspoon extra-virgin olive oil

Lemon Dill Sauce

1 tablespoon butter

1 tablespoon all-purpose (plain) flour

¾ cup (180 ml) dry white wine

¾ cup (180 ml) heavy (double) cream

Juice of ½ lemon

2 tablespoons coarsely chopped fresh dill

Salt and freshly ground black pepper

Serves: 4
Preparation: 45 minutes + time for pasta
Cooking: 15 minutes
Level: 3

BEEF RAVIOLI WITH PUMPKIN SAUCE

Cook the pasta in a large pot of salted, boiling water until al dente. • Meanwhile, heat the cream and nutmeg in a medium frying pan over medium-high heat until reduced by half. • Stir in the pumpkin purée, sour cream, and Parmesan. • Drain the pasta and add to the pan with the sauce. • Toss gently. • Garnish with the chives and shavings of Parmesan. • Serve hot.

1   pound (500 g) beef-filled ravioli

1   cup (250 ml) heavy (double) cream

1/2 teaspoon freshly grated nutmeg

2   cups (350 g) pumpkin or winter squash purée

5   tablespoons sour cream

1/4 cup (30 g) freshly grated Parmesan cheese

24 fresh chives, cut into short lengths

    Shavings of Parmesan cheese, to serve

Serves: 4
Preparation: 5 minutes
Cooking: 10 minutes
Level: 1

■ ■ ■ *You can make the pumpkin purée at home by boiling or steaming 12 ounces (350 g) of pumpkin until tender, then mashing it with a fork.*

VEGETABLE LASAGNA STACKS WITH PESTO

Pesto: Combine the garlic, pine nuts, basil leaves, and Parmesan in a food processor and process until coarsely chopped. • With the motor running, gradually add the oil and process until the mixture becomes a smooth paste.

Lasagna: Cut the pasta sheets into twelve 3-inch (8-cm) squares. • Cook the pasta in a large pot of salted, boiling water until al dente. • Drain well. • Arrange one sheet of pasta in the center of each plate. Top with a couple of spinach leaves, a slice each of tomato and mozzarella, a basil leaf, and a spoonful of pesto. • Top with another sheet of lasagna and layer as before, finishing with a layer of lasagna. Each stack should have two complete layers. • Place a generous spoonful of pesto on top of each stack and serve hot.

Pesto

2 cloves garlic

2 tablespoons pine nuts, toasted

Large bunch fresh basil leaves

2 tablespoons freshly grated Parmesan cheese

1/2 cup (125 ml) extra-virgin olive oil

Lasagna

14 ounces (400 g) fresh lasagna sheets

2 ounces (60 g) baby spinach leaves

4 large vine tomatoes, cut into thick slices

3 balls of mozzarella, cut into thick slices

8 fresh basil leaves

Serves: 4
Preparation: 40 minutes
Cooking: 5 minutes
Level: 2

■ ■ ■ *If you are short of time, use 12 sheets of dried lasagna cooked according to the instructions on the package.*

ROASTED SQUASH AND ROSEMARY LASAGNA

Preheat the oven to 425°F (220°C/ gas 7). • Peel the squash and discard the seeds. Cut into $1/2$-inch (1 cm) cubes. • Mix the squash in a large bowl with the rosemary, garlic, and oil. Season with salt and pepper and toss well. • Spoon the mixture into a baking dish. • Roast for about 25 minutes, or until golden brown. • Meanwhile, heat the milk in a saucepan over low heat. Remove from the heat just before it comes to a boil. • Melt the butter in a medium saucepan. Add the flour and stir with a wooden spoon. • Remove from the heat and add $1/4$ cup (60 ml) of the hot milk. Beat well with a whisk to prevent lumps from forming. Gradually pour in the remaining milk, whisking constantly. • Return to the heat and bring to a boil over low heat. Cook, stirring constantly, until the sauce has thickened, about 5 minutes. • Add the roasted squash mixture and mix well. • Oil a baking dish (about 9 x 13 inches/

1	small butternut squash
2	large sprigs fresh rosemary
3	cloves garlic, finely chopped
2	tablespoons extra-virgin olive oil
	Salt and freshly ground black pepper
4	cups (1 liter) milk
1/4	cup (60 g) butter
4	tablespoons all-purpose (plain) flour
1	pound (500 g) dried lasagna sheets
1	cup (125 g) freshly grated Parmesan cheese
1	cup (250 ml) heavy (double) cream
1/2	cup (60 g) freshly grated Parmesan cheese, to serve

Serves: 6–8
Preparation: 35 minutes
Cooking: 1 hour
  40 minutes
Level: 3

23 x 33 cm) and ladle just enough sauce over the bottom to cover it. • Cook the lasagna sheets in salted, boiling water for the time indicated on the package. Gently squeeze out excess moisture and place on a clean kitchen towel. • Place a layer of lasagna sheets over the sauce and spread with more sauce. Sprinkle with Parmesan and cover with another layer of lasagna. Repeat this layering process until all the sauce, lasagna, and Parmesan has been used, finishing with a layer of pasta. • Season the cream with salt and beat until it begins to thicken. • Spread the cream over the lasagna. • Sprinkle with the extra Parmesan and cover with aluminum foil. • Lower the heat to 350°F (180°C/gas 4) and bake for 30 minutes. • Discard the foil and bake until golden brown, about 15 minutes more. • Remove from the oven and let stand for 5 minutes. • Serve hot.

See photograph on the following page

SPINACH AND RICOTTA CANNELLONI

Preheat the oven to 350°F (180°C/gas 4).
• Cook the pasta in salted, boiling water
for 2 minutes. • Drain, rinse, and dry on
kitchen towels. • Sauté the onion in 2
tablespoons of butter in a large frying pan
over medium heat until golden, about 5
minutes. • Add the flour and cook, stirring,
for 1 minute. • Remove from the heat and
gradually stir in the milk. • Return to the
heat and bring to a boil, stirring constantly.
• Add the chives and lemon juice. Season
with salt and pepper. Set aside. • Sauté the
spinach in the remaining 1 tablespoon of
butter in a small frying pan over medium
heat until wilted, 2–3 minutes. • Mix the
spinach, ricotta, parsley, and basil in a
small bowl. • Spoon a little of the mixture
onto each sheet of pasta and roll up like
jelly rolls (Swiss rolls). • Spoon the
tomatoes into a square baking dish. •
Place the cannelloni on top, pour the sauce
over the top, and sprinkle with the bread
crumbs and Parmesan. • Bake for 30–35
minutes, until golden. • Serve hot.

8	ounces (250 g) dried lasagna sheets
1	onion, finely chopped
3	tablespoons butter
3	tablespoons all-purpose (plain) flour
2	cups (500 ml) milk
1	tablespoon snipped fresh chives
	Juice of 1/2 lemon
	Salt and freshly ground black pepper
1	cup (250 g) cooked spinach
1	cup (250 g) fresh ricotta cheese
1	teaspoon finely chopped fresh parsley
1	teaspoon finely chopped fresh basil
1	(14-ounce/400-g) can chopped tomatoes, drained
2	tablespoons fresh white bread crumbs
5	tablespoons freshly grated Parmesan cheese

Serves: 4
Preparation: 30 minutes
Cooking: 50 minutes
Level: 2

PRUNE GNOCCHI

Soak the prunes in warm water for 30 minutes. • Drain. Pit the prunes and fill each cavity with $1/2$ teaspoon of sugar. • Cook the potatoes in salted, boiling water until tender, about 25 minutes. Mash until smooth. Spread out on a chopping board and season with salt. Let cool. • Add the flour, egg, and 1 tablespoon of butter to the potatoes. Use your hands to mix the potato mixture until well blended. • Shape the dough into dumplings about the size of golf balls. Insert a prune into the center of each one. • Cook the gnocchi in small batches in a large pot of salted, boiling water until they bob up to the surface, 4–5 minutes each batch. • Remove with a slotted spoon, drain well, and transfer to a heated serving dish. • Fry the bread crumbs in the remaining butter and sugar in a small frying pan until browned. Dust with the cinnamon. Sprinkle over the gnocchi and serve hot.

30 prunes

$1/2$ cup (100 g) sugar

Salt

2 pounds (1 kg) potatoes, peeled

$1 2/3$ cups (250 g) all-purpose (plain) flour

1 large egg

2 tablespoons melted butter

2 tablespoons fine dry bread crumbs

$1/2$ teaspoon ground cinnamon

Serves: 6
Preparation: 20 minutes
+ 30 minutes to soak
Cooking: 30–40 minutes
Level: 3

SPINACH AND RICOTTA GNOCCHI WITH TOMATO SAUCE

236

Mix the ricotta and spinach in a large bowl. • Add the eggs, Parmesan, and 1/2 cup (75 g) of flour. Season with salt and pepper and add the lemon zest. • Dip your hands in the remaining flour and shape the mixture into 2-inch (5-cm) gnocchi. • Cook the gnocchi in a large pot of salted, boiling water until they bob up to the surface, 8–10 minutes per batch. • Remove with a slotted spoon and transfer to individual serving dishes. • Cover with the tomato sauce and sprinkle with the Parmesan. • Serve at once.

2 cups (500 g) fresh ricotta cheese, drained

Scant 1 1/2 cups (350 g) cooked spinach, finely chopped

2 large eggs, lightly beaten

1 cup (125 g) freshly grated Parmesan cheese

Scant 2/3 cup (90 g) all-purpose (plain) flour

Salt and freshly ground black pepper

Grated zest of 1/2 lemon

2 cups (500 ml) store-bought or homemade tomato sauce (see Cavatelli with Pancetta and Sun-Dried Tomatoes, page 190)

2 ounces (60 g) Parmesan cheese, shaved, to serve

Serves: 4
Preparation: 30 minutes
Cooking: 20 minutes
Level: 2

GNOCCHI ALLA ROMANA

Bring the milk to a boil in a large saucepan. • Gradually sprinkle in the semolina, stirring constantly to prevent lumps from forming. • Simmer, stirring constantly, until the mixture is thick, about 15 minutes. • Remove from the heat and season with salt. • Stir in half the butter, the egg yolks, half the Parmesan, and the Gruyère. • Spread the mixture out to a thickness of 1/2-inch (1-cm) on a lightly floured work surface. Let cool. • Use a glass to cut out rounds. • Preheat the oven to 350°F (180°C/gas 4). • Butter four individual baking dishes. • Use the pieces leftover after cutting out the disks to form a first layer in the dishes. Sprinkle with some Parmesan. Lay the rounds over the top, one overlapping the next. • Melt the remaining 1/4 cup (60 g) butter and pour over the top. Sprinkle with the remaining 1/2 cup (60 g) of Parmesan and season with white pepper. • Bake until golden, about 30 minutes. • Serve hot.

4 cups (1 liter) milk

1²/₃ cups (250 g) semolina

Salt and freshly ground white pepper

1/2 cup (125 g) butter

2 large egg yolks

1 cup (125 g) freshly grated Parmesan cheese + extra, to serve

6 tablespoons freshly grated Gruyère cheese

Serves: 4
Preparation: 10 minutes + 30 minutes to cool
Cooking: 45 minutes
Level: 2

RICE AND GRAINS

RICE WITH SEAFOOD

Soak the mussels and clams in cold water for 1 hour. • Scrub the mussels thoroughly, removing any beards and discarding broken shells. Rinse well. • Sauté the mussels and clams in a large frying pan over high heat until they have all opened, about 10 minutes. • Discard any that do not open. Set aside. • Bring the fish stock to a boil in a large saucepan. • Sauté the onion in 2 tablespoons of the oil in a large saucepan over medium heat until softened, about 5 minutes. • Add the garlic and chile and sauté for 1 minute. • Add the squid and cook over medium heat for 5 minutes. • Add the tomatoes and season with salt and pepper. • Continue cooking over low heat for 5 minutes. • Toast the rice in the remaining 2 tablespoons oil in a medium frying pan over high heat for 1 minute. • Add the rice to the squid mixture. • Add the wine and cook until

2	pounds (1 kg) mussels, in shell
2	pounds (1 kg) clams, in shell
6	cups (1.5 liters) fish stock (see page 243)
1	onion, finely chopped
1/4	cup (60 ml) extra-virgin olive oil
2	cloves garlic, finely chopped
1	dried red chile, crumbled
1	pound (500 g) squid, scored
6	tomatoes, peeled and diced
	Salt and freshly ground black pepper
2	cups (400 g) short-grain risotto rice
1/4	cup (60 ml) dry white wine
1 3/4	pounds (800 g) shrimp (prawns)
1/4	cup (60 ml) water
2	tablespoons butter
2	tablespoons finely chopped fresh parsley

Serves: 6–8
Preparation: 20 minutes
 + 1 hour to soak
Cooking: 45 minutes
Level: 2

evaporated. • Pour in enough stock to generously cover the rice. Lower the heat, cover, and cook for 10–15 minutes, or until the rice is tender. • Add the shrimp, mussels, and clams and cook until heated through. • Stir in the butter. • Serve hot, garnished with the parsley.

243

Fish Stock

1	pound (500 g) heads and bones mixed fish
3	quarts (3 liters) cold water
1	carrot, chopped
1	stalk celery, chopped
1	onion, chopped
1	shallot
1	bunch parsley
4	black peppercorns
1/2	cup (125 ml) dry white wine
1	clove garlic
1	sprig thyme
1	tablespoon coarse sea salt

Fish Stock: Soak the fish heads and bones in a large bowl of cold water for 1 hour. This will remove any traces of blood. • Drain and put in a large saucepan with the water over medium heat. Bring to a boil, then add all the other ingredients. Simmer for about 1 1/2 hours. Filter the stock through a fine-mesh strainer before use.

■ ■ ■ *This recipe will make about 8 cups (2 liters) of fish stock. It will keep in the refrigerator for 3 to 4 days and can be frozen for up to 3 months.*

See photograph on the following page

RICE WITH PEAS AND PESTO

Cook the rice in a large pot of salted boiling water until tender, 12–15 minutes. • Boil the peas in salted water until tender, about 5 minutes. • Sauté the onion in the butter in a large frying pan over medium heat until softened, about 5 minutes. • Drain the rice and peas and add to the pan with the onion and parsley. Season with salt and pepper. Sauté over high heat for 1 minute. • Spoon into heated serving dishes and top with the pesto. • Serve hot.

2 cups (400 g) short-grain rice

1 cup (150 g) frozen peas

1 onion, finely chopped

1/3 cup (90 g) butter, cut up

Salt and freshly ground black pepper

2 tablespoons finely chopped fresh parsley

1 cup (250 ml) pesto (see Vegetable Lasagna Stacks with Pesto, page 226)

Serves: 4
Preparation: 10 minutes
Cooking: 20 minutes
Level: 1

RICE WITH MOZZARELLA AND HERBS

Cook the rice in a large pot of salted, boiling water until tender, 12–15 minutes. • Drain well and return to the pot. • Stir in the butter, mixed herbs, mozzarella, and Parmesan. Season with salt and pepper and stir until the mozzarella is melting. • Serve hot.

1½ cups (300 g) short-grain rice

⅓ cup (90 g) butter, cut up

2 tablespoons finely chopped mixed fresh herbs, such as basil, chives, and parsley

8 ounces (250 g) mozzarella cheese, diced

½ cup (60 g) freshly grated Parmesan cheese

Salt and freshly ground black pepper

Serves: 4
Preparation: 5 minutes
Cooking: 15–20 minutes
Level: 1

■ ■ ■ *Substitute the same quantity of Gorgonzola cheese for the mozzarella for a slightly different but equally delicious dish.*

SPRING VEGETABLE RISOTTO

Clean the artichokes by pulling the tough outer leaves down and snapping them off. Cut off the top third of the leaves and trim the stalk. Cut in half and use a sharp knife to remove any fuzzy choke. Slice thinly and drizzle with the lemon juice. • Sauté the onion, celery, and parsley in the oil and 3 tablespoons of butter in a large, deep frying pan over medium heat for about 5 minutes, or until softened. • Add the carrot, potatoes, artichokes, and tomatoes and season with salt. Sauté for 3 minutes. • Add 1/2 cup (125 ml) of the stock. • Simmer over low heat until the potatoes and the carrots begin to soften, about 10 minutes. • Add the peas, green beans, spinach, and asparagus. • Add the rice and stir for 2 minutes. • Begin stirring in the vegetable stock, 1/2 cup (125 ml) at a time. Cook and stir until each addition has been absorbed, and the rice is tender, 15–18 minutes. • Remove from

2	artichokes
	Freshly squeezed juice of 1 lemon
1	**medium onion, finely chopped**
1	**stalk celery, finely chopped**
4	**tablespoons finely chopped fresh parsley**
2	**tablespoons extra-virgin olive oil**
6	**tablespoons (90 g) butter, cut up**
1	**large carrot, diced**
2	**potatoes, peeled and diced**
3	**large firm-ripe tomatoes, peeled and diced**
	Salt
4	**cups (1 liter) vegetable stock (see page 251), boiling**
2	**cups (300 g) frozen peas**
4	**ounces (125 g) green beans, cut into short lengths**
3	**cups (150 g) spinach leaves, finely shredded**

8   ounces (250 g)
     asparagus, cut into
     short lengths
2   cups (400 g) short-
     grain risotto rice
2   tablespoons freshly
     grated Parmesan
     Freshly ground black
     pepper

Serves: 4–6
Preparation: 20 minutes
Cooking: 40 minutes
Level: 2

Vegetable Stock
2   tablespoons extra-
     virgin olive oil
2   medium onions,
     studded with
     2 cloves
2   carrots, chopped
2   stalks celery, with
     leaves
2   tomatoes
     Small bunch fresh
     parsley
6   black peppercorns
2   bay leaves
1   teaspoon salt
10   cups (2.5 liters)
     water

the heat and stir in the Parmesan and
the remaining 3 tablespoons butter.
Season with pepper. • Serve hot.

■ ■ ■ *Arborio, Vialone Nano, and Carnaroli are the*
three classic types of Italian rice used to make
risottos. The trick to making good risotto lies in
toasting the rice in a little oil and butter before adding
the hot stock a little at a time, then stirring constantly
as it cooks, to release the starches in the rice.

Vegetable Stock: Heat the oil in a large
saucepan over medium heat. Add the
onions, carrots, celery, tomatoes, parsley,
peppercorns, bay leaves, and salt. Sauté
for 5 minutes. • Pour in the water,
partially cover the pan, and bring to a
boil. Simmer for 1 hour. • Pour through
a strainer, discarding the vegetables.

See photograph on the following page

■ ■ ■ *Vegetable stock is light and tasty and very easy*
to make. It will keep for 4–5 days in the refrigerator
and freezes well. This recipe will make about 8 cups
(2 liters). Freeze any leftover stock for later use.

SAFFRON AND CHICKEN RISOTTO

Bring the chicken stock and wine to a boil in a large saucepan. Add the saffron. Decrease the heat and keep warm. • Brown the chicken in the oil in a large, deep frying pan over medium heat for 5 minutes. • Remove the chicken from the pan and set aside. • Add the butter and leeks to the same pan. Simmer over low heat, stirring often, until the leeks are very tender and golden, about 25 minutes. • Add the rice and cook for 3 minutes, stirring constantly. • Begin stirring in the stock, 1/2 cup (125 ml) at a time. Cook and stir until each addition has been absorbed and the rice is very tender, 15–18 minutes. • Stir in the chicken. Season with pepper and cook for 2 minutes more. • Serve hot, topped with the Parmesan and basil.

4 cups (1 liter) chicken stock (see Leek and Potato Soup, page 158)

1/2 cup (125 ml) dry white wine

Pinch of saffron strands

2 boneless, skinless chicken breast halves, cut into thin strips

1 tablespoon extra-virgin olive oil

3 tablespoons butter

3 leeks, finely sliced

2 cups (400 g) short-grain risotto rice

Freshly ground black pepper

2 ounces (60 g) Parmesan cheese, shaved

Sprigs of fresh basil, to garnish

Serves: 4–6
Preparation: 10 minutes
Cooking: 1 hour
Level: 2

LEMON AND BROCCOLI RISOTTO

Sauté the onion and garlic in the oil in a large, deep frying pan over medium heat until the garlic turns pale gold, about 3 minutes. • Stir in the rice and cook for 3 minutes, stirring constantly. • Stir in the wine and when this has been absorbed, begin stirring in the vegetable stock, 1/2 cup (125 ml) at a time. Cook and stir until each addition has been absorbed and the rice is tender, 15–18 minutes. • Add the broccoli 3 minutes before the end of the cooking time. • Remove from the heat. Stir in the parsley and lemon zest and juice. Season with pepper. Cover and let stand for 3 minutes. • Serve hot.

■ ■ ■ *Cut the lemon zest into fine shreds by removing the outer yellow layer of the lemon with a lemon zester. If you don't have a lemon zester, grate the zest finely.*

1	onion, finely chopped
1	clove garlic, finely chopped
1	tablespoon extra-virgin olive oil
1 1/2	cups (300 g) short-grain risotto rice
1/2	cup (125 ml) dry white wine
4	cups (1 liter) vegetable stock (see page 251), boiling
1	small head broccoli, cut into florets
2	tablespoons finely chopped fresh parsley
	Zest and juice of 1 organic lemon
	Freshly ground black pepper

Serves: 4
Preparation: 20 minutes
Cooking: 25 minutes
Level: 2

BABY SPINACH AND GORGONZOLA RISOTTO

Sauté the onion and garlic in the oil in a large, deep frying pan over medium heat until the garlic turns pale gold, about 3 minutes. • Stir in the rice and cook for 3 minutes, stirring constantly. • Stir in the wine and when this has been absorbed, begin stirring in the vegetable stock, 1/2 cup (125 ml) at a time. Cook and stir until each addition has been absorbed and the rice is tender, 15–18 minutes. • Remove from the heat and stir in the spinach and Gorgonzola. Season with salt and pepper. Cover and let stand for 3 minutes. • Serve hot.

1   small onion,
    finely chopped

2   cloves garlic,
    finely chopped

2   tablespoons extra-
    virgin olive oil

2   cups (400 g) short-
    grain risotto rice

1/2 cup (125 ml) dry
    white wine

4   cups (1 liter)
    vegetable stock
    (see page 251),
    boiling

5   cups (250 g)
    baby spinach

8   ounces (250 g)
    Gorgonzola cheese,
    diced

    Salt and freshly
    ground black pepper

Serves: 4–6
Preparation: 30 minutes
Cooking: 25 minutes
Level: 2

ROASTED GARLIC AND CAPACOLLO RISOTTO

Preheat the oven to 400°F (200°C/ gas 6). • Blanch the fava beans in a pot of boiling water, 2–3 minutes. Drain well and set aside. • Place the garlic bulb on a baking sheet lined with aluminum foil and drizzle with 1 teaspoon of the oil. Wrap and seal. Roast for 1 hour. • Remove the garlic from the oven and squeeze out the individual garlic cloves from the skin. Set aside. • Dice the capacollo. • Sauté the onion and capacollo in the 1 remaining tablespoon of oil in a large, deep frying pan over medium heat for 3 minutes. • Add the rice and cook for 3 minutes, stirring constantly. • Stir in the garlic and wine and when the wine has been absorbed, begin stirring in the chicken stock, 1/2 cup (125 ml) at a time. Cook and stir until each addition has been absorbed and the rice is tender, 15–18 minutes. • Stir in the butter, Parmesan, and fava beans 3 minutes before the rice is cooked. • Season with salt and pepper. Serve hot.

2 cups (250 g) fresh fava (broad) beans

1 bulb garlic

14 thin slices capacollo or prosciutto (Parma ham)

1 small onion, finely chopped

1 tablespoon + 1 teaspoon extra-virgin olive oil

2 cups (400 g) short-grain risotto rice

2 tablespoons dry white wine

6 cups (1.5 liters) chicken stock (see Leek and Potato Soup, page 158), boiling

2 tablespoons butter

3 tablespoons freshly grated Parmesan cheese

Salt and freshly ground black pepper

Serves: 4–6
Preparation: 35 minutes
Cooking: 1 hour
    25 minutes
Level: 2

PUMPKIN, LEMON, AND PARMESAN RISOTTO

Bring the vegetable stock to a boil in a large saucepan. Add the saffron. Decrease the heat and keep warm.
• Sauté the onion and garlic in the oil and butter in a large, deep frying pan over medium heat until the garlic turns pale gold, about 3 minutes. • Stir in the rice and pumpkin and cook for 3 minutes, stirring constantly. • Stir in the wine and when this has been absorbed, begin stirring in the stock, 1/2 cup (125 ml) at a time. Cook and stir until each addition has been absorbed and the rice is tender, 15–18 minutes. • Season with salt and pepper. • Remove from the heat. Stir in the lemon zest and juice. • Serve hot, garnished with the rosemary and Parmesan.

4	cups (1 liter) vegetable stock (see page 251)
1/4	teaspoon saffron strands
1	onion, finely chopped
1	clove garlic, finely chopped
2	tablespoons extra-virgin olive oil
1	tablespoon butter
2	cups (400 g) short-grain risotto rice
2	pounds (1 kg) pumpkin or butternut squash, seeded and diced
3/4	cup (180 ml) dry white wine
	Salt and freshly ground black pepper
	Grated zest and juice of 1 lemon
2	ounces (60 g) Parmesan cheese, shaved
1/2	teaspoon fresh rosemary, to garnish

Serves: 4–6
Preparation: 20 minutes
Cooking: 30 minutes
Level: 2

RISOTTO WITH TOMATO AND BASIL

Sauté the onion in 2 tablespoons of butter in a medium saucepan over medium heat until softened, about 3 minutes. • Stir in the tomatoes and simmer until the tomatoes have broken down, about 15 minutes. • Melt 2 tablespoons of the remaining butter in a large, deep frying pan over high heat. • Add the rice and cook for 3 minutes, stirring constantly. • Pour in the wine and cook until it evaporates. • Add the tomato sauce and basil. • Begin stirring in the vegetable stock, ½ cup (125 ml) at a time. Cook and stir until each addition has been absorbed and the rice is tender, 15–18 minutes. • Remove from the heat Stir in the remaining 2 tablespoons butter and the Parmesan. Season with salt and pepper. • Cover and let stand for 1 minute. • Garnish with the basil leaves and serve hot.

1   small onion, finely chopped

1/3 cup (90 g) butter, cut up

2   cups (500 g) peeled and chopped tomatoes

2   cups (400 g) short-grain risotto rice

1/3 cup (90 ml) dry white wine

3   cups (750 ml) vegetable stock (see page 251), boiling

20 fresh basil leaves, torn + extra to garnish

2   tablespoons freshly grated Parmesan cheese

Salt and freshly ground black pepper

Serves: 4–6
Preparation: 15 minutes
Cooking: 40 minutes
Level: 2

SEAFOOD PAELLA WITH ORANGES

Preheat the oven to 400°F (200°C/ gas 6). • Sauté the garlic in the oil in a paella pan or large frying pan about 18 inches (45 cm) in diameter over medium heat until it turns pale gold, about 3 minutes. • Discard the garlic. • Add the rice and cook for 3 minutes, stirring constantly. • Pour in the fish stock and bring to a boil. Simmer, stirring frequently for 15–20 minutes, until the rice is almost cooked. • Add the shrimp, peas, scallops, and fish. Season with salt and pepper. Add the bay leaf and saffron. Simmer over medium heat until the liquid has almost all been absorbed and the seafood is cooked. The rice grains should still be slightly crunchy and there should still be some liquid in the pan. • Stir in the slices of orange. Bake in the oven, uncovered, for 10 minutes. • Cover the pan with aluminum foil or parchment paper and let stand for 10 minutes. • Remove the bay leaf and garnish with the dill. Serve hot.

3 cloves garlic, peeled

1/4 cup (60 ml) extra-virgin olive oil

3 cups (600 g) short-grain rice

6 cups (1.5 liters) boiling fish stock (see page 243)

2 pounds (1 kg) shrimp (prawns)

1 cup (150 g) frozen peas

1 pound (500 g) scallops, shucked

1 pound (500 g) firm white fish, such as cod or monkfish, diced

Salt and freshly ground black pepper

1 bay leaf

10 strands saffron

1 organic orange, with peel, thinly sliced

Fresh dill, to garnish

Serves: 6–8
Preparation: 25 minutes + 10 minutes to stand
Cooking: 30 minutes
Level: 2

VEGETABLE COUSCOUS

Place the couscous in a large bowl. Pour in the boiling water. Let stand for 15 minutes, or until the couscous has absorbed the water. • Break the couscous up with a fork. • Sauté the garlic and cumin in the oil in a large frying pan over medium heat until aromatic, about 2 minutes. • Add the eggplant and bell pepper. Cook until the eggplant starts to soften, 3–4 minutes. • Add the fennel, dates, and wine. Cook, stirring occasionally, until the vegetables are cooked 5–10 minutes. • Mix the vegetable mixture, parsley, and lemon zest and juice into the couscous. • Warm over low heat for 5 minutes. • Serve hot.

2 cups (400 g) couscous

2 cups (500 ml) boiling water

1 clove garlic, finely chopped

1 teaspoon cumin seeds

1 tablespoon extra-virgin olive oil

1 eggplant (aubergine), diced

1 red bell pepper (capsicum), seeded and diced

1 bulb fennel, thinly sliced

6 dates, pitted and chopped

1/2 cup (125 ml) dry white wine or Marsala

3 tablespoons finely chopped fresh parsley

Finely grated zest and juice of 1 lemon

Serves: 4–6
Preparation: 20 minutes
   + 15 minutes to stand
Cooking: 20 minutes
Level: 1

BAKED BASIL
AND GARLIC POLENTA

Preheat the oven to 350°F (180°C/gas 4).
• Butter a 7 x 11-inch (25 x 20-cm)
baking dish. • Pour the chicken stock into
a saucepan and bring to a boil. •
Gradually pour in the polenta, stirring
constantly until it starts to come away
from the sides of the pan, 8–10 minutes.
• Remove from the heat and stir in the
garlic, basil, and pecorino. Season with
salt and pepper. • Pour the polenta
evenly into the prepared dish. • Bake
for 30 minutes. • Serve the polenta cut
into triangles.

6 cups (1.5 liters) chicken stock (see Leek and Potato Soup, page 158)

2 cups (300 g) instant polenta

1 clove garlic, finely chopped

2 tablespoons fresh basil, torn

1 cup (120 g) freshly grated pecorino cheese

Salt and freshly ground black pepper

Serves: 4
Preparation: 15 minutes
Cooking: 35–40 minutes
Level: 1

■ ■ ■ Instant or quick-cooking polenta usually takes
8–10 minutes cooking on the stovetop, as opposed to
45–50 minutes using regular polenta. If preferred, use
the regular variety, which is simply cornmeal.

POLENTA WITH MUSHROOM SAUCE

Bring the water to a boil in a large saucepan. Add the sea salt and 1 tablespoon of oil. • Gradually sprinkle in the polenta, stirring constantly with a wooden spoon to prevent lumps from forming. • Continue cooking over medium heat, stirring almost constantly, until it starts to come away from the sides of the pan, 45–50 minutes.
• Meanwhile, cut the large mushrooms in half, leaving the smaller ones whole.
• Sauté the garlic, onion, and pancetta in the remaining oil in a large frying pan until the garlic turns pale gold, about 3 minutes. • Add the mushrooms and season with salt and pepper. Cover and simmer over low heat for 20 minutes, stirring often. • Add the marjoram.
• Spoon the polenta into individual serving plates. Spoon the mushrooms and their cooking juices over the top.
• Serve hot.

8	cups (2 liters) water
1	tablespoon salt
5	tablespoons extra-virgin olive oil
2²/₃	cups (400 g) polenta
1	clove garlic, finely chopped
1	red onion, chopped
³/₄	cup (90 g) diced pancetta
1	pound (500 g) chanterelle or white mushrooms
	Salt and freshly ground black pepper
2	tablespoons fresh marjoram

Serves: 4
Preparation: 30 minutes
Cooking: 1 hour 10 minutes
Level: 2

BAKED POLENTA WITH RICOTTA AND TOMATO

Preheat the oven to 350°F (180°C/gas 4). • Press the ricotta through a fine-mesh strainer. • Sauté the onion in the oil and lard in a large frying pan over medium heat until softened, about 5 minutes. • Stir in the parsley and tomatoes. Season with salt and pepper. Simmer over low heat for 15 minutes. • Thickly slice the polenta and arrange a layer in an oiled baking dish. Add half the ricotta and spoon one-third of the sauce over the top. Sprinkle with pecorino. Add another layer of polenta, the remaining ricotta, and half of the remaining sauce. Sprinkle with pecorino and then cover with the remaining polenta. Cover with the remaining sauce and sprinkle with the remaining pecorino. • Bake for 20–25 minutes until golden brown. • Serve warm with the arugula, if liked.

1   cup (250 g) fresh ricotta cheese

1   medium onion, finely chopped

3   tablespoons extra-virgin olive oil

3   tablespoons lard or butter, cut up

3   tablespoons finely chopped fresh parsley

1   (14-ounce/400-g) can tomatoes, with juice

    Salt and freshly ground black pepper

1   pound (500 g) precooked polenta

1/2 cup (60 g) freshly grated pecorino or Parmesan cheese

    Arugula (rocket), to serve (optional)

Serves: 6–8
Preparation: 20 minutes
Cooking: 40 minutes
Level: 2

■ ■ ■ *Precooked polenta is available, usually in tubes, in specialty food stores, ready to be sliced and baked.*

CABBAGE STUFFED WITH GRAINS

Preheat the oven to 350°F (180°C/gas 4). • Toast the bread crumbs until lightly browned, about 10 minutes. Set aside. • Increase the oven temperature to 375°F (190°C/gas 5). • Remove the large outer leaves from the cabbages. Set aside twelve well-formed leaves. Cut the remaining cabbage and core into quarters. Shred enough cabbage to yield 2 cups (400 g). • Sauté the shallot and half the carrot in ¼ cup (60 g) of butter in a medium saucepan over medium heat for 1 minute. • Add the cabbage and sauté for 3 minutes. • Stir in the rice and buckwheat groats. Sauté for 2 minutes. • Add 2½ cups (625 ml) of the chicken stock and the tomato paste. Season with salt and pepper. Bring to a boil. Cover, decrease the heat to low, and cook for 15 minutes. The grains will be almost tender. • Let cool slightly, then stir in the parsley. • In a roasting pan or straight-sided frying pan just large enough to hold twelve cabbage rolls side by side,

⅓	cup (20 g) fresh white bread crumbs
2	medium red cabbages
1	shallot, finely chopped
2	medium carrots, finely grated
½	cup (125 g) butter
½	cup (50 g) long-grain white rice
½	cup (50 g) buckwheat groats or quinoa
4	cups (1 liter) chicken stock (see Leek and Potato Soup, page 158)
1	cup (250 ml) tomato paste (concentrate)
1	teaspoon salt
1	teaspoon freshly ground black pepper
3	tablespoons finely chopped fresh parsley
2	onions, finely chopped
2	stalks celery, thinly sliced

2 tablespoons extra-virgin olive oil

3 cups (750 ml) dry white wine

2 tablespoons red wine vinegar

Serves: 6
Preparation: 10 minutes
Cooking: 1 hour
    20 minutes
Level: 3

sauté the onions, celery, and the remaining carrots in 2 table-spoons of butter and oil over medium heat until softened, about 3 minutes. • Add the wine and the remaining 1½ cups (375 ml) of chicken stock. • Simmer for 15 minutes. • Remove from the heat and set aside. • Bring a large pot of salted water to a boil. • Add the vinegar. • Parboil the reserved cabbage leaves until slightly softened, 3–5 minutes. • Remove with a slotted spoon. • When cool enough to handle, cut away the center rib of each leaf to make them easier to roll. • Place 1 tablespoon of the stuffing near the bottom of each leaf. Roll up halfway, then fold in the sides and continue rolling to make a short, fat log. Place seam-side down in the pan. • Melt the remaining 2 tablespoons butter and brush over the cabbage rolls. Sprinkle with the bread crumbs. Cover and bake for 15 minutes. • Uncover and bake for 15 minutes more. • Serve hot.

See photograph on the following page

ROASTED TOMATOES WITH LEMON-HERB COUSCOUS

Preheat the oven to 350°F (180°C/gas 4).
• Using a sharp knife, carefully cut the top off each tomato, then scoop out the flesh, taking care not to pierce the skin. Finely chop the tomato flesh and set aside. • Mix the butter, vegetable stock, and the juice and zest of the lemons in a medium saucepan and bring to a boil. Season with salt and pepper. • Remove from the heat and add the couscous, herbs, and reserved tomato flesh.
• Let stand for 15 minutes, or until the couscous has absorbed the water.
• Break the couscous up with a fork.
• Carefully spoon the couscous mixture into each tomato cavity, filling them to the top. • Place the tomatoes close together in a baking dish. • Bake for 20–30 minutes until the tomatoes have softened and the mixture is warm.
• Serve hot.

8   medium tomatoes
2   tablespoons butter
1   cup (250 ml) vegetable stock (see page 251)
    Juice and grated zest of 3 lemons
    Salt and freshly ground black pepper
2$1/2$ cups (250 g) couscous
4   tablespoons finely chopped mixed fresh herbs, such as parsley, dill, cilantro (coriander), basil

Serves: 6–8
Preparation: 20 minutes
    + 15 minutes to stand
Cooking: 20–30 minutes
Level: 2

SPANISH-STYLE STUFFED BELL PEPPERS

Stuffed Bell Peppers: Preheat the oven to 350°F (180°C/gas 4). • Choose six bell peppers for filling. Carefully slice the tops off. Remove the seeds and membranes from inside each bell pepper, leaving a cavity for filling. Set aside. • Finely dice the remaining two bell peppers. • Sauté the onion, leek, and garlic in the oil in a large frying pan over medium heat until golden, about 5 minutes. • Add the diced bell peppers and tomatoes and cook for 10 minutes. • Stir in the rice, then add the hot vegetable stock and saffron. Season with salt and pepper. Bring to a boil and simmer, uncovered, for 20 minutes. • Stir in the almonds, currants, zucchini, cumin, and paprika.

Stuffed Bell Peppers

- 8 large bell peppers (capsicums), mixed colors
- 1 onion, finely chopped
- 1 leek, finely sliced and rinsed
- 1 clove garlic, finely chopped
- 3 tablespoons extra-virgin olive oil
- 2 tomatoes, finely chopped
- 1 cup (200 g) long-grain rice
- 3 cups (750 ml) vegetable stock (see page 251), hot
- Pinch of saffron strands
- Salt and freshly ground black pepper
- 1/4 cup (30 g) slivered almonds, toasted
- 1/4 cup (30 g) currants
- 4 medium zucchini (courgettes), diced
- 1 teaspoon ground cumin
- 1 tablespoon sweet paprika

Tomato Sauce

2   leeks, thinly sliced

1   tablespoon extra-
    virgin olive oil

2   pounds (1 kg)
    tomatoes, coarsely
    chopped

1   cup (250 ml) dry
    red wine

2   tablespoons honey

    Salt and freshly
    ground black
    pepper

Serves: 6
Preparation: 50 minutes
Cooking: 1 hour
   30 minutes
Level: 3

Tomato Sauce: Sauté the leeks in the oil in a medium saucepan over medium heat until softened, about 3 minutes. • Add the tomatoes, red wine, and honey. Season with salt and pepper. Simmer for 15 minutes. Set aside. • Spoon the rice mixture evenly into the bell peppers, mounding it if necessary to use all the mixture. • Place the bell peppers in a baking dish that is small enough to hold them all snugly. • Spoon the tomato sauce over the top. • Bake until the bell peppers are softened, 30–35 minutes. • Serve hot.

■ ■ ■ *You can vary this recipe by stuffing different vegetables, such as tomatoes, round zucchini, or onions (or a mixture of them all). If using zucchini or onions, parboil them for 5 minutes before stuffing and baking.*

See photograph on the following page

MOROCCAN-STYLE STUFFED MUSHROOMS

Plump the raisins in hot water for 5 minutes. • Cook the rice in a large pot of salted boiling water until tender, 12–15 minutes. • Remove from the heat, add the spinach, and mix well. Cover and let stand for 10 minutes. • Preheat the oven to 400°F (200°C/gas 6). • Remove the stalks from the mushrooms and chop them. • Sauté the chopped mushroom stalks, onion, and garlic in the oil in a large frying pan over medium heat for 2 minutes, until softened. • Stir in the raisins, pine nuts, parsley, cilantro, cumin, coriander, and cinnamon. Season with salt and pepper. • Mix in the spinach and rice. • Fill the mushroom caps with the mixture. Place in a baking dish. • Bake for 30 minutes. • Serve hot.

1/4 cup (45 g) golden raisins (sultanas)

1 cup (200 g) long-grain rice

1 cup (50 g) baby spinach, finely shredded

8 large mushrooms

1 onion, chopped

1 clove garlic, chopped

3 tablespoons extra-virgin olive oil

1/4 cup (45 g) pine nuts, toasted

1 tablespoon coarsely chopped fresh parsley

1 tablespoon coarsely chopped fresh cilantro (coriander)

1 teaspoon ground cumin

1 teaspoon ground coriander

Pinch of cinnamon

Salt and freshly ground black pepper

■ ■ ■ *Portobello mushrooms are ideal for this recipe.*

Serves: 4
Preparation: 30 minutes
Cooking: 50 minutes
Level: 2

EGGPLANT PROVENÇAL

Cut the eggplant in half lengthwise.
• Scoop out the flesh, leaving a 1-inch
(2.5 cm) shell, and dice. Sprinkle the
shells with salt and let drain for 30
minutes. • Preheat the oven to 350°F
(180°C/gas 4). • Sauté the diced
eggplant, shallots, garlic, and tomato in
1 tablespoon of oil in a large frying pan
for 5 minutes. • Stir in the rice and
oregano. Season with salt and pepper.
• Pat dry the eggplant shells with paper
towels and brush the outside of the
shells with the remaining 1 tablespoon
of oil. • Spoon the rice mixture evenly
into the eggplants. Arrange in a shallow
ovenproof dish and pour the tomato juice
over the top. • Bake for 35–40 minutes
until the eggplant is tender. • Sprinkle
with the parsley and serve hot.

2	medium eggplant (aubergines)
	Salt
4	shallots, finely chopped
1	clove garlic, finely chopped
1	tomato, diced
2	tablespoons extra-virgin olive oil
2	cups (400 g) cooked rice
1/2	teaspoon dried oregano
	Salt and freshly ground black pepper
1	cup (250 ml) tomato juice
1	tablespoon finely chopped fresh parsley

Serves: 4
Preparation: 15 minutes
   + 30 minutes to drain
Cooking: 40–45 minutes
Level: 2

STUFFED ZUCCHINI WITH TOMATO AND PECORINO

Tomato Salsa: Mix the tomatoes, onion, chiles, parsley, lemon juice, and oil in a small bowl. Let stand for 1 hour.
• Preheat the oven to 400° (200°C/gas 6). • Cook the rice in a large pot of salted, boiling water until tender, 12–15 minutes. • Remove from the heat. Cover and let stand for 10 minutes. Fluff up the rice with a fork.

Zucchini: Cut the zucchini in half lengthwise. Scoop out the centers with a teaspoon and discard. Season the zucchini with salt and let drain for 10 minutes. Rinse and pat dry with paper towels. • Mix the rice, tomato salsa, and chicken in a medium bowl. Season with paprika, salt, and pepper. • Spoon the mixture into the zucchini and top with the pecorino. • Place in a baking dish. Pour the water into the dish and drizzle the zucchini with oil. • Bake until the chicken is cooked and the cheese has melted, about 30 minutes. • Serve hot.

Tomato Salsa

4 tomatoes, diced
1 onion, chopped
2 green chilies, seeded and diced
3 tablespoons finely chopped parsley
  Juice of 1/2 lemon
3 tablespoons extra-virgin olive oil

Zucchini

1 cup (200 g) short-grain rice
4 medium zucchini (courgettes)
8 ounces (250 g) ground (minced) chicken
1 teaspoon sweet paprika
  Salt and freshly ground black pepper
1/2 cup (60 g) freshly grated pecorino cheese
1/4 cup (60 ml) water
2 tablespoons extra-virgin olive oil

Serves: 4
Preparation: 45 minutes + 1 hour to stand
Cooking: 50 minutes
Level: 2

SEAFOOD

SEAFOOD BRUSCHETTA

Soak the clams and mussels in cold water for 1 hour. Scrub the mussels. • Preheat the oven to 400°F (200°C/gas 6). • Place the shellfish in a large frying pan over medium heat and cook until they open. Discard any that do not open. • Remove the clams and mussels from their shells. • Heat 2 tablespoons of oil in a large frying pan over medium heat and sauté the parsley and half the chopped garlic for 2–3 minutes. • Turn the heat to high and add the shrimp and squid and sauté for 5 minutes (not longer or the squid will become leathery). Set aside. • In a separate pan, heat 2 tablespoons of oil with the remaining chopped garlic and tomatoes and simmer for 10 minutes. • Add the clams and mussels, season with salt and pepper, and simmer until the shellfish are cooked, 2–3 minutes. • Toast the bread in the oven until crisp and golden brown. • Rub the toast with the whole cloves of garlic and drizzle with the remaining oil. • Top with the seafood and serve warm.

8	ounces (250 g) clams, in shell
8	ounces (250 g) mussels, in shell
5	tablespoons extra-virgin olive oil
6	tablespoons finely chopped fresh parsley
6	cloves garlic, 4 finely chopped, 2 whole
4	ounces (125 g) shrimp (prawn tails), peeled and deveined
4	ounces (125 g) squid, cleaned and coarsely chopped
4	tomatoes, peeled and finely chopped
	Salt and freshly ground black pepper
8	slices firm-textured bread

Serves: 4
Preparation: 30 minutes
  + 1 hour to soak
Cooking: 25 minutes
Level: 2

BOUILLABAISSE

Remove the bones and skin from the fish fillets and cut into 1-inch (2.5-cm) cubes. If using shrimp (prawns), peel and devein them, leaving the tails intact. • Heat the oil in a large saucepan over medium heat. Add the garlic, onions, and leeks and sauté until the onions are softened, about 5 minutes. • Add the tomatoes, thyme, basil, parsley, bay leaves, orange zest, saffron, wine, and stock and bring to a boil. Reduce the heat and simmer for 30 minutes. • Add the fish and seafood and simmer until tender and cooked, about 10 minutes. Season with salt and pepper and serve hot.

4 pounds (2 kg) mixed firm fish fillets or steaks, such as monkfish, gurnard, scorpionfish, halibut, cod, snapper, sea bass, grouper, rockfish

2 pounds (1 kg) mixed seafood, such as shrimp (prawns), lobster, octopus, crab, squid rings, scallops, cleaned

1/4 cup (60 ml) extra-virgin olive oil

2 cloves garlic, finely chopped

2 large onions, chopped

2 leeks, sliced

2 (14-ounce/400-g) cans diced tomatoes, with juice

1 tablespoon finely chopped fresh thyme

2 tablespoons finely chopped fresh basil

2 tablespoons finely chopped fresh parsley

2 bay leaves

2 tablespoons finely grated orange zest

1 teaspoon saffron threads

1 cup (250 ml) dry white wine

8 cups (2 liters) fish stock (see page 243) or water, boiling

Salt and freshly ground black pepper

Serves: 8–12
Preparation: 30 minutes
Cooking: 45 minutes
Level: 2

Rouille

6 cloves garlic, peeled

1/2 teaspoon salt

1/2 teaspoon saffron threads, crumbled

2 large egg yolks

1 cup (250 ml) extra-virgin olive oil

■■■ *Bouillabaisse is a famous fish soup from Provence. It is made with a combination of fish and seafood cooked in a broth made from onions, garlic, olive oil, tomatoes, parsley, saffron, and fish stock or water. There are many versions, and if you don't live in the Mediterranean region, you will have to use local fish and seafood. Traditionally, the broth is strained and served as a soup, usually ladled over toast rubbed with garlic, while the fish and seafood are served later as a second course. If liked, serve it all together as a hearty stew. However you decide to serve it, be sure to offer it with rouille (saffron garlic sauce). See our simple recipe below.*

Rouille: Combine the garlic, salt, saffron, and egg yolks in a food processor and process briefly. • With the motor running, add the oil slowly in a thin, steady stream, processing until it is thick and creamy.

See photograph on the following page

SARDINIAN FISH STEW

Heat the oil in a large saucepan over medium heat. Add the onions, bell peppers, and chopped garlic and sauté until softened, about 5 minutes. • Add the tomatoes and wine, bring to a boil, then simmer until the mixture reduces a little, about 5 minutes. • Add the firmer seafood and season with salt and pepper. Simmer for 5 minutes, stirring frequently. • Add the more delicate fish and enough water to cover and simmer until the fish flakes easily when tested with the tip of a sharp knife, about 5 minutes. Stir in the fresh herbs, reserving a little for the garnish. • Rub the toast with the remaining whole clove of garlic and place a slice in each soup bowl. Ladle the soup over the top, garnish with the reserved herbs, and serve hot.

■■■ *If you prefer, add clams and mussels to this soup along with the fish. Simmer until the shellfish open, then remove the mollusks from their shells, returning them to the soup.*

1/3	cup (90 ml) extra-virgin olive oil
2	onions, sliced
2	green bell peppers (capsicums), sliced
4	cloves garlic, 3 finely chopped, 1 whole
1	(14-ounce/400-g) can tomatoes, with juice
1/2	cup (125 ml) dry white wine
4	pounds (2 kg) mixed firm white fish fillets or steaks, such as John Dory, sea bass, flounder, cod, ling, monkfish, grouper, tilapia
	Salt and freshly ground black pepper
4	tablespoons mixed chopped fresh herbs, such as parsley, marjoram, dill, oregano
6	slices firm Italian-style bread, toasted

Serves: 6
Preparation: 15 minutes
Cooking: 20 minutes
Level: 2

MARINATED BABY OCTOPUS

Mix the oil, lemon zest, lemon juice, shallots, and oregano in a large bowl. Season with salt and pepper. Add the octopus and toss gently in the marinade. Set aside to marinate for 1 hour. • Heat a grill pan over high heat, lightly brushing it with oil. Add the octopus, and cook—basting with the marinade—until tender, 2–3 minutes. • Serve hot or at room temperature on the salad greens.

1/2 cup (125 ml) extra-virgin extra-virgin olive oil

Finely grated zest of 1 lemon

2 tablespoons freshly squeezed lemon juice

4 shallots, finely sliced

2 teaspoons finely chopped fresh oregano

Salt and freshly ground black pepper

1 1/2 pounds (750 g) baby octopus, cleaned

Salad greens, to serve

Serves: 6
Preparation: 5 minutes
+ 1 hour to marinate
Cooking: 3 minutes
Level: 1

SHRIMP WITH VEGETABLES

Heat 2 tablespoons of oil in a medium saucepan over medium heat. Add the onion and sauté until softened, about 5 minutes. Add the bell pepper, garlic, and tomatoes and simmer for 7 minutes. • Add the asparagus, spinach, wine, and lemon juice and season with salt and pepper. Cover and simmer gently until the spinach and asparagus are tender, 5–10 minutes. Remove from the heat and keep warm. • Heat the remaining 1/4 cup (60 ml) of oil in a large frying pan over high heat. Add the shrimp and sauté until just cooked, about 3 minutes. • Add the shrimp to the spinach mixture, stirring well. Serve hot.

1/4 cup (60 ml) + 2 tablespoons extra-virgin olive oil

1 medium onion, diced

1 red bell pepper (capsicum), seeded and diced

1 clove garlic, finely chopped

2 tomatoes, peeled and diced

1 bunch spinach, coarsely chopped

1 bunch asparagus, cut into 1/2-inch (1-cm) pieces

2 tablespoons dry white wine

Freshly squeezed juice of 1 lemon

Salt and freshly ground black pepper

1 pound (500 g) shrimp (prawn tails), shelled and deveined

Serves: 4
Preparation: 15 minutes
Cooking: 20–25 minutes
Level: 2

MUSSELS WITH ROASTED TOMATO SAUCE

Soak the mussels in cold water for 1 hour. Rinse well and scrub off any beards with a wire brush. Discard any mussels that are open. • Preheat the oven to 375°F (190°C/gas 5). • Place the tomatoes, cut side up, on a baking sheet. Drizzle with 2 tablespoons of oil and season with salt. • Roast in the oven until softened, 15–20 minutes. Cut into large pieces. • Heat the remaining 1/4 cup (60 ml) of oil in a saucepan and sauté the garlic and the onion until softened, about 5 minutes. • Add the white wine and simmer for 2 minutes. • Add the canned tomatoes, tomato paste, fish stock, and oregano. Simmer for 10 minutes. • Add the roasted tomatoes. Season with salt and pepper. Add the mussels, cover, and simmer until the mussels have opened, about 5 minutes. Discard any that do not open. • Serve hot with crusty fresh bread.

2 1/2 pounds (1.2 kg) mussels, in shell

6 medium, ripe tomatoes, halved

1/4 cup (60 ml) + 2 tablespoons extra-virgin olive oil

Salt

4 cloves garlic, finely chopped

1 onion, chopped

1/3 cup (90 ml) dry white wine

1 (14-ounce/400-g) can tomatoes, with juice

1/4 cup (60 g) tomato paste

1/3 cup (90 ml) fish stock (see page 243) or water

2 tablespoons finely chopped fresh oregano

Freshly ground black pepper

Crusty bread, to serve

Serves: 4–6
Preparation: 30 minutes
   + 1 hour to soak
Cooking: 40 minutes
Level: 2

PAN-FRIED SQUID WITH LEMON

Cut each squid tube open along one side. With a sharp knife score inside the skin diagonally in both directions. Cut the squid into rectangles measuring about 1 x 2 inches (2 x 5 cm). • Combine the semolina, salt, and pepper in a small bowl. • Heat the oil in a large frying pan or wok over high heat. • Dip the squid into the semolina mixture, turning to coat well. • Fry in small batches until lightly brown and crisp, 3–4 minutes each batch. • Drain on paper towels. • Serve hot with the lemon wedges.

$1^1/2$ **pounds (750 g) squid tubes**

$^2/3$ **cup (100 g) fine semolina**

1 **teaspoon salt**

1 **teaspoon freshly ground black pepper**

1 **cup (250 ml) extra-virgin olive oil, to fry**

1 **lemon, cut into wedges**

Serves: 4–6
Preparation: 15 minutes
Cooking: 15–20 minutes
Level: 2

SHRIMP WITH FETA CHEESE

Heat the butter and oil in a medium saucepan over medium heat. Add the onion and sauté until softened, about 5 minutes. • Add the wine, tomatoes, garlic, and oregano. Season with salt and pepper. Bring to a boil, then simmer until the sauce reduces a little, 8–10 minutes. • Add the cheese, mix well, and simmer for 10 minutes, stirring occasionally. • Add the shrimp and simmer until tender, about 5 minutes. Do not overcook. • Garnish with the oregano leaves and serve hot.

1	tablespoon butter
1	tablespoon extra-virgin olive oil
1	small onion, finely chopped
1/2	cup (125 ml) dry white wine
4	tomatoes, peeled, seeded, and chopped
1	clove garlic, finely chopped
2	teaspoons finely chopped fresh oregano + extra leaves, to garnish
	Salt and freshly ground black pepper
4	ounces (125 g) feta cheese, crumbled
2	pounds (1 kg) shrimp (prawn tails), peeled, and deveined

Serves: 4
Preparation: 10 minutes
Cooking: 25 minutes
Level: 2

WARM SALAD OF MONKFISH AND SHRIMP

Mix ¼ cup (60 ml) of oil, 1 teaspoon salt, lemon juice, peppercorns, fennel seeds, and red pepper in a shallow dish. Add the monkfish, turn once or twice, and set aside to marinate for 1 hour. • Heat the remaining 1 tablespoon of oil in a large frying pan over high heat. Take the fish fillets out of the marinade and cook until lightly browned, 2 minutes on each side. Keep warm. • Add the shrimp to the pan and toss over high heat until cooked through and lightly browned, about 2 minutes. Remove and keep warm. • Remove the pan from the heat and add the sherry vinegar and the marinade and let it bubble as the heat dissipates. Add the clarified butter, tomato, and chervil. Season with salt and pepper. • Arrange the endive, fish, and shrimp on four serving plates and spoon the sherry and butter dressing over the top. Serve hot.

■■■Clarified butter is easy to make. Melt the butter slowly, then let sit for a few minutes to separate. Skim off the foam that rises to the top and gently pour the butter off the milk solids, which will have settled on the bottom.

5	tablespoons extra-virgin olive oil
	Salt and freshly ground black pepper
1	tablespoon freshly squeezed lemon juice
½	teaspoon crushed black peppercorns
½	teaspoon crushed fennel seeds
½	teaspoon crushed red pepper flakes
4	ounces (125 g) thin monkfish fillets, membranes removed
12	jumbo shrimp (prawns), peeled and deveined
3	tablespoons sherry vinegar
½	cup (125 g) clarified butter
1	large tomato, peeled and diced
2	tablespoons chopped fresh chervil
2	heads Belgian endive (witlof/chicory)

Serves: 4
Preparation: 30 minutes
  + 1 hour to marinate
Cooking: 10 minutes
Level: 2

MUSSELS WITH FENNEL AND SPINACH SAUCE

Soak the mussels in cold water for 1 hour. Rinse well and remove any beards. Discard any mussels that are open. • Heat the oil in a medium saucepan over medium heat. Add the fennel, onion, and garlic and sauté for 5 minutes. • Add the chicken stock, cover, and simmer until fennel has softened, 5–10 minutes. Strain, reserving the cooking liquid. • Put the strained ingredients in a food processor, with 1 cup (250 ml) of the reserved liquid and process until finely chopped. Add the parsley and spinach. Process until smooth. • Pour the fennel mixture in a saucepan and bring to a gentle boil. Add the cream and simmer until the mixture starts to thicken, 1–2 minutes. Stir in the sour cream and season with salt and pepper. • Combine the mussels and white wine in a large saucepan and cover. Simmer until the mussels open, about 5 minutes. • Remove the top shells from the mussels. Spoon the fennel and spinach sauce over the top and serve.

2　pounds (1 kg) mussels, in shell

2　tablespoons extra-virgin olive oil

2　small bulbs fennel, finely chopped

1　onion, finely sliced

2　cloves garlic, finely chopped

2　cups (500 ml) chicken stock (see Leek and Potato Soup, page 158)

2　tablespoons finely chopped fresh parsley

4　cups (200 g) chopped spinach leaves

1/2　cup (125 ml) heavy (double) cream

1/4　cup (60 ml) sour cream

　Salt and freshly ground black pepper

1/2　cup (125 ml) dry white wine

Serves: 4
Preparation: 15 minutes
　+ 1 hour to soak
Cooking: 25–30 minutes
Level: 2

GRILLED SCALLOPS WITH ORANGE SALSA

Slice the top and bottom off 1 orange, then cut away the peel and pith, following the curve of the fruit. Cut between the membranes to release the segments, then chop coarsely. • Squeeze the juice of the second orange into a bowl, add the chopped orange, tomatoes, garlic, vinegar, and 3 tablespoons of the oil. Season with salt and pepper and set aside. • Heat a grill pan over medium-high heat. Brush both sides of each fennel slice with half the remaining oil. Grill until tender and charred, 2–3 minutes on each side. Transfer to four serving plates and keep warm. • Brush the scallops with the remaining oil and cook for 1 minute, then turn and grill until cooked through, about 30 seconds. • Top each portion of fennel with 1 tablespoon of crème fraîche, three scallops, and the salsa. Sprinkle with the arugula and serve hot.

2	small oranges
4	sun-dried tomatoes in oil, drained and chopped
1	clove garlic, finely chopped
1	tablespoon balsamic vinegar
5	tablespoons extra virgin extra-virgin olive oil
	Salt and freshly ground black pepper
1	large bulb fennel, quartered and thinly sliced
12	fresh sea scallops
1/4	cup (60 ml) crème fraîche or sour cream
	Handful of arugula (rocket) leaves, to serve

Serves: 4
Preparation: 15 minutes
Cooking: 10 minutes
Level: 2

SHRIMP WITH SAUCE VERTE

Sauce Verte: Steam the spinach until just tender, about 1 minute. Cool quickly in cold water, drain, and squeeze dry. Chop coarsely with a knife. • Put the mayonnaise in a bowl. Add the spinach, parsley, chives, and dill and mix to combine.

Shrimp: Combine the vermouth, scallions, parsley sprig, and bay leaf in a saucepan over medium heat. Season with salt and pepper. Bring to a gentle boil. Add the shrimp and simmer until pink, 2–3 minutes. Drain, discarding everything except the shrimp.

To serve, smear a little sauce in a circle on four entrée plates. Arrange the shrimp on the sauce, garnish with the salad greens, and serve hot.

Sauce Verte
- 12 spinach leaves, stems removed
- 3/4 cup (180 ml) mayonnaise
- 4 tablespoons finely chopped fresh parsley
- 2 tablespoons snipped fresh chives
- 1 tablespoon finely chopped fresh dill

Shrimp
- 3/4 cup (180 ml) dry vermouth
- 6 scallions (spring onions), coarsely chopped
- 1 sprig fresh parsley
- 1 bay leaf
- Salt and freshly ground black pepper
- 1 1/2 pounds (750 g) shrimp (prawn tails), peeled and deveined
- Mixed salad greens, to garnish

Serves: 4
Preparation: 12 minutes
Cooking: 10 minutes
Level: 2

CHERMOULA SHRIMP

Soak 12 small bamboo skewers in cold water for 30 minutes. • Thread two shrimp onto each skewer. Place the shrimp skewers in a single layer in a shallow dish. • Combine the onion, garlic, cilantro, mint, parsley, chile, cumin, paprika, lime juice, and oil in a food processor. Process until smooth. • Coat the shrimp with this mixture, cover with plastic wrap (cling film), and chill in the refrigerator for 3–4 hours. • Heat a grillpan or barbecue over high heat. Cook the shrimp until tender, 3–5 minutes. • Serve hot with the salad greens and lime wedges.

24 large shrimp (prawn tails), about 1 1/2 pounds (750 g), peeled and deveined

1/4 small mild red or yellow onion, coarsely chopped

2 cloves garlic, peeled

3 tablespoons chopped fresh cilantro (coriander)

3 tablespoons chopped fresh mint leaves

3 tablespoons chopped fresh parsley

1 small fresh red chile, seeded and chopped

1 teaspoon ground cumin

1/2 teaspoon sweet paprika

2 tablespoons freshly squeezed lime juice

2 tablespoons extra-virgin olive oil

Salad greens and lime wedges, to serve

■■■ *Chermoula (or charmoula) is a marinade used in North African cooking. It is made from a mixture of oil, lemon or lime juice, herbs, and spices and is used to marinate meat and fish before grilling.*

Serves: 4–6
Preparation: 10 minutes
+ 3–4 hours to chill
Cooking: 15 minutes
Level: 2

BAKED SCALLOPS WITH PROSCIUTTO

Preheat the oven to 450°F (230°C/gas 8).
• Heat 1 tablespoon of oil in a large frying pan and sauté the scallops over high heat for 1 minute. • Place each scallop back in a small ramekin or scallop shell and season with salt and pepper. Cover each one with a piece of prosciutto. • Combine the bread crumbs, parsley, lemon juice, and remaining 3 tablespoons of oil in a small bowl. • Sprinkle over the scallops. • Place the ramekins or shells on a baking sheet and bake until just tender, about 5 minutes. • Serve hot.

$1/4$ cup (60 ml) extra-virgin olive oil

1 pound (500 g) sea scallops

Salt and freshly ground black pepper

4 slices prosciutto, cut into squares about the size of the scallops

$1/2$ cup (60 g) fine dry bread crumbs

1 tablespoon finely chopped fresh parsley

1 teaspoon freshly squeezed lemon juice

Serves: 4
Preparation: 5 minutes
Cooking: 5–10 minutes
Level: 1

■■■ *These scallops look pretty when served in their shells. Fresh scallops in their shells are not always easy to find. If you do find them, rinse well and serve the scallops in them.*

CLAMS WITH POTATOES

Soak the clams in a large bowl of cold water for one hour. Rinse well. • Heat the oil in a large frying pan over medium heat. Add the onion and sauté until softened, about 5 minutes. Add the tomatoes and sauté for 5 minutes. • Transfer to a large saucepan, add the potatoes and water and bring to a boil. • Place the clams in a large frying pan with the wine and cook over medium heat until they open, about 5 minutes. Discard any that haven't opened. • Meanwhile, very finely chop the garlic with the parsley, saffron, and a little salt. Place in a small bowl and stir in 1 tablespoon of the liquid from the clams. Mix well and stir into the potatoes with the rest of the clam liquid (keep the clams to one side). Cover and simmer until the potatoes are done, 15–20 minutes.
• Add the clams and serve hot.

1	pound (500 g) small clams, in shell
1/4	cup (60 ml) extra-virgin olive oil
1	medium onion, diced
2	medium tomatoes, peeled, seeded, and chopped
2	pounds (1 kg) potatoes, peeled and cut into small chunks
3	cups (750 ml) water
1/4	cup (60 ml) white wine
1	clove garlic, coarsely chopped
1	tablespoon chopped fresh parsley
5	strands of saffron
	Salt

Serves: 4
Preparation: 15 minutes
  + 1 hour to soak
Cooking: 50 minutes
Level: 2

GARLIC SHRIMP

Put the shrimp in a shallow dish.
• Combine the garlic, chile, oil, lemon juice, and pepper in a small bowl. Pour this mixture over the shrimp and let marinate for 20 minutes. • Heat the marinade in a large frying pan over medium-high heat. Cook the shrimp for about 3 minutes on each side, according to size, until pink and cooked through.
• Place in individual serving dishes or on a large platter. Pour the juices from the pan over the shrimp. Garnish with the lime and serve hot.

2　pounds (1 kg) shrimp (prawn tails), peeled and deveined

4　cloves garlic, finely chopped

1　small fresh red chile, seeded and finely chopped

1/4　cup (60 ml) extra-virgin olive oil

Freshly squeezed juice of 2 lemons

Freshly ground black pepper

Lime wedges, to garnish

Serves: 6
Preparation: 10 minutes
　+ 20 minutes to
　marinate
Cooking: 6–8 minutes
Level: 1

FISH TAGINE WITH RAISINS AND HONEY

Combine 5 tablespoons of oil, cumin, 1/2 teaspoon of cinnamon, cayenne pepper, saffron, and salt in a small bowl. Rub into the fish fillets on both sides. Place on a plate, cover, and chill in the refrigerator for 2 hours for the flavors to penetrate. • Heat the remaining 1 tablespoon of oil in a large frying pan over medium heat and sear the fish on both sides until lightly colored. Remove immediately and set aside. • Add the diced onion to the pan and sauté until softened, about 5 minutes. • Stir in the black pepper, remaining 1/2 teaspoon of cinnamon, honey, vinegar, raisins, and parsley. Turn the heat down to low and simmer for 10 minutes. • Return the fish to the pan, spoon some sauce over the top, cover, and simmer for 5 minutes, basting occasionally with sauce. • Serve hot.

■■■ Serve this flavorful dish with freshly cooked rice or couscous.

1/3	cup (90 ml) extra-virgin olive oil
1	teaspoon ground cumin
1	teaspoon ground cinnamon
1/4	teaspoon cayenne pepper
1/4	teaspoon powdered saffron
1/2	teaspoon salt
1 1/2	pounds (750 g) firm white fish fillets, such as sea bass, flounder, cod, ling, monkfish, grouper
1	large mild red onion, finely diced
1/4	teaspoon black pepper
1/4	cup (60 ml) honey
1/4	cup (60 ml) wine vinegar
3/4	cup (135 g) raisins, soaked and drained
2	tablespoons finely chopped fresh parsley

Serves: 4
Preparation: 5 minutes
 + 2 hours to marinate
Cooking: 25 minutes
Level: 1

SMOKED SALMON CARPACCIO

Combine the oil, lemon juice, and capers in a bowl and whisk until well combined. • Arrange the smoked salmon and onion on serving plates. • Drizzle the dressing over the smoked salmon, sprinkle with the parsley, and top with pepper, if liked.

1/4 cup (60 ml) extra-virgin olive oil

3 tablespoons freshly squeezed lemon juice

2 teaspoons small whole capers

12 ounces (350 g) smoked salmon, about 3–4 slices per person

1 small mild red onion, thinly sliced

1 tablespoon coarsely chopped fresh parsley

Freshly ground black pepper (optional)

Serves: 4
Preparation: 10 minutes
Level: 1

TUNA STEAKS WITH YOGURT AND CUCUMBER SAUCE

Combine the yogurt, mayonnaise, lime juice, cucumber, and grapes in a small bowl and set aside. • Mix the butter and lemon juice together. Brush the tuna steaks with this mixture. • Preheat a grill pan over medium heat. • Add the tuna steaks and grill until cooked through, about 4 minutes on each side. • Transfer the tuna to serving plates. Top with yogurt and cucumber sauce and garnish with the salad greens and tomatoes.

1/2 cup (125 ml) plain low-fat yogurt

3 tablespoons mayonnaise

1 tablespoon freshly squeezed lime juice

2 tablespoons grated cucumber

4 ounces (125 g) green seedless grapes, chopped

2 tablespoons melted butter

1/4 cup (60 ml) freshly squeezed lemon juice

4 tuna steaks, weighing about 6 ounces (180 g) each

Salad greens, to serve

Cherry tomatoes, halved, to serve

Serves: 4
Preparation: 10 minutes
Cooking: 20 minutes
Level: 1

TUNA CARPACCIO IN BELGIAN ENDIVE

Carpaccio: Using a very sharp knife, cut the fish into paper-thin slices. This will be easier to do if you place the fish in the freezer for 10 minutes before slicing. • Place the thinly sliced tuna onto individual serving plates and sprinkle with endive, radicchio, capers, and onion.

Lime and Horseradish Dressing: Combine the oil, lime juice, sherry, and horseradish relish in a small bowl. • Whisk to combine. • Drizzle the dressing over the fish. • Serve immediately.

■■■ *If you prefer, replace the tuna with the same amount of fresh swordfish or kingfish fillets, or use a combination of all three.*

Carpaccio

8   ounces (250 g) very fresh tuna, in a single large piece

4   heads Belgian endive (witlof/chicory), leaves separated

1   head red radicchio, leaves separated

1   mild red onion, diced

1   tablespoon capers, drained

Lime and Horseradish Dressing

2   tablespoons extra-virgin olive oil

2   tablespoons freshly squeezed lime juice

1   tablespoon sherry or wine vinegar

1   teaspoon horseradish relish

Serves: 6
Preparation: 10 minutes + 10 minutes to freeze
Level: 1

SALMON EN CROUTE WITH HERB SAUCE

Salmon: Preheat the oven to 425°F (220°C/gas 7). • Place the salmon fillets on a large dish or platter. Season with salt and pepper and put in the refrigerator. • Cut the pastry into 6 equal pieces, each one large enough to wrap easily around a salmon fillet. They should be at least twice as large as the fillets. Place on a dampened baking sheet and prick well with a fork. Refrigerate for 15 minutes. • Sprinkle each piece of pastry with a little semolina. Lay a salmon fillet on top close to one edge, dot with butter, and sprinkle with lemon zest and juice, dill, parsley, and tarragon. Season with salt and pepper. Fold the pastry over to enclose the fillet, tucking in the ends and folding the edges underneath. Make 2–3 neat cuts in the top of each package so that steam can escape during baking. Brush with the egg mixture. • Bake for 15 minutes, then turn the heat down to 300°F (150°C/gas 2). Bake for 15 more minutes. Cover with aluminum foil if the pastry starts to burn.

Salmon

6	skinless salmon fillets, about 8 ounces (250 g) each
	Salt and freshly ground black pepper
1	pound (500 g) puff pastry, thawed, if frozen
2	tablespoons semolina
1	tablespoon butter, cut up
	Finely grated zest and juice of 1/2 lemon
1	tablespoon finely chopped fresh dill
1	tablespoon finely chopped fresh parsley
1	tablespoon finely chopped fresh tarragon
1	large egg yolk beaten with 1 tablespoon milk, to glaze

Herb Sauce

3 tablespoons butter

1 tablespoon all-purpose (plain) flour

3/4 cup (200 ml) fish stock (see page 243)

3 tablespoons dry white wine

1 tablespoon heavy (double) cream

1 tablespoon finely chopped fresh dill

1 tablespoon finely chopped fresh parsley

1 tablespoon finely chopped fresh tarragon

Salt and freshly ground black pepper

Serves: 6
Preparation: 40 minutes + 15 minutes to chill
Cooking: 40 minutes
Level: 3

Herb Sauce: Melt half the butter in a small saucepan. Add the flour and stir for 1 minute. Add the fish stock and wine and bring to a boil, stirring constantly. • Simmer, stirring often, until thickened, about 5 minutes. • Add the cream, dill, parsley, and tarragon and season with salt and pepper. Whisk in the remaining butter. • Serve the salmon hot with the sauce passed separately.

■■■ *En croute is a French term meaning "baked in a pastry crust."*

See photograph on the following page

CRAB AU GRATIN

Crabmeat Mixture: Preheat the oven to 400°F (200°C/gas 6). • Melt the butter in a small frying pan over medium heat. Add the shallot and mushrooms, season with salt and pepper, and sauté until softened, about 5 minutes. Stir in the Cognac and crabmeat and remove from the heat.

Gratin Sauce: Melt the butter in a medium saucepan over low heat. Add the flour and stir for 1–2 minutes. Gradually add the fish stock, stirring constantly until the sauce thickens, about 5 minutes. • Stir in the cream and mustard and season with the cayenne pepper. Simmer for 2–3 minutes then remove from the heat. Stir in the crabmeat and mushroom mixture. • Spoon the mixture into 4 small baking dishes (about 1 cup/250 ml capacity). Sprinkle each one with 2 tablespoons of cheese. • Bake for about 10 minutes, until bubbling and golden brown on top. • Serve hot.

Crabmeat Mixture

1 tablespoon butter

1 shallot, finely chopped

2 medium white mushrooms, finely chopped

Salt and freshly ground black pepper

2 tablespoons Cognac

12 ounces (350 g) fresh crabmeat

Gratin Sauce

2 tablespoons butter

2 tablespoons all-purpose (plain) flour

1 1/2 cups (375 ml) fish stock (see page 243)

1/2 cup (125 ml) heavy (double) cream

1 teaspoon Dijon mustard

1 teaspoon cayenne pepper

1/2 cup (60 g) freshly grated Parmesan cheese

Serves: 4
Preparation: 20 minutes
Cooking: 25 minutes
Level: 2

PAN-FRIED SARDINES WITH MIXED HERBS

Place the eggs in a bowl and whisk lightly. • Combine the flour, bread crumbs, Parmesan, herbs, pepper, and salt on a large plate. • Dip the sardine fillets into the beaten eggs. Dredge in the flour mixture, pressing the mixture firmly onto the fish. • Heat the oil in a large frying pan over medium-high heat. Fry the sardines 4 at a time until crisp and golden brown, 1–2 minutes each side. • Serve hot with the lemon wedges and extra fresh herbs, and couscous, if liked.

■■■ *Fresh sardines are truly delicious. To prepare this dish you will need gutted sardines, with heads and backbones removed, which have been opened out flat. Ask you fish vendor to prepare them for you. If you prefer to prepare them yourself begin by snapping off the fishes' heads and then pulling them straight down; most of the entrails will come away with the heads. Use your fingers to remove any remaining innards. Grasp the backbone and gently pull it out of each fish. Carefully open the fish out until flat.*

2   large eggs

1/3   cup (50 g) all-purpose (plain) flour

1   cup (150 g) fine dry bread crumbs

1/4   cup (30 g) freshly grated Parmesan cheese

3   tablespoons mixed fresh herbs (parsley, basil, oregano and marjoram), coarsely chopped + extra, to serve

1/2   teaspoon freshly ground black pepper

  Salt

3   pounds (1.5 kg) sardines, cleaned (see note below)

1/2   cup (125 ml) extra-virgin olive oil

2   lemons, cut into wedges

  Freshly cooked couscous, to serve (optional)

Serves: 6
Preparation: 15 minutes
Cooking: 10 minutes
Level: 2

SALMON CUTLETS WITH DILL HOLLANDAISE SAUCE

Salmon Cutlets: Combine the oil, lemon juice, salt, and pepper in a ceramic dish. Add the salmon cutlets, turing them in the mixture to coat. Let marinate for 4 hours.

Dill Hollandaise Sauce: Mix the vinegar, pepper, and water in a small saucepan. Bring to a boil, then simmer until only 1 tablespoon of the liquid is left. • Combine the egg yolks and vinegar mixture in a food processor and process for 1 minute. • With the motor still running, gradually add the hot melted butter and process until thick. • Add the lemon juice and dill and season with salt and pepper. Keep warm. • Lightly oil and heat a grill pan or preheat a broiler (grill). Grill the salmon cutlets until cooked through, 2–3 minutes each side. • Blanch the asparagus in salted boiling water until just tender, 2–3 minutes. Drain well. • Serve the salmon hot with the sauce and asparagus on the side.

Salmon Cutlets

3   tablespoons extra-virgin olive oil + extra, for the grill

1   tablespoon freshly squeezed lemon juice

    Salt and freshly ground black pepper

4   salmon cutlets, about 8 ounces (250 g) each

1   bunch asparagus, to serve

Dill Hollandaise Sauce

1/3   cup (90 ml) white wine vinegar

    Freshly ground black pepper

1/4   cup (60 ml) water

4   large egg yolks

3/4   cup (200 g) butter, melted

3   tablespoons freshly squeezed lemon juice

3   tablespoons finely chopped fresh dill

Serves: 4
Preparation: 15 minutes + 4 hours to marinate
Cooking: 10 minutes
Level: 1

SWORDFISH KEBABS WITH TOMATO SAUCE

Tomato Sauce: Heat the oil in a medium saucepan over medium heat and sauté the onion and garlic until softened, about 5 minutes. • Add the tomatoes and sugar and season with salt and pepper. Simmer gently for 20 minutes. Add the basil and keep warm.

Kebabs: Soak the bamboo skewers in cold water for 30 minutes. • Preheat a grill pan (or barbecue) to medium. • Cut the swordfish, bell pepper, and eggplant into large cubes. • Thread alternate pieces of fish and vegetables onto the skewers. • Combine the oil with the rosemary in a small bowl. Season with salt and pepper. • Brush the kebabs with some of the oil mixture and place on the grill. Cook, turning over at least once to brown on all sides. Baste with the oil mixture as the kebabs cook. The swordfish should be golden, with vegetables slightly charred, 5–10 minutes. • Serve hot with the sauce.

Tomato Sauce

1   tablespoon extra-virgin olive oil

1   onion, finely chopped

2   cloves garlic, finely chopped

2   (14-ounce/400-g) cans tomatoes, with juice

1/2   teaspoon sugar

Salt and freshly ground black pepper

8   fresh basil leaves, torn

Kebabs

1 1/2   pounds (750 g) swordfish steak

1   green bell pepper (capsicum), seeded

1   eggplant (aubergine), with skin

1/2   cup (125 ml) extra-virgin olive oil

1   tablespoon chopped fresh rosemary

Serves: 4–6
Preparation: 20 minutes
Cooking: 30 minutes
Level: 2

SALMON IN VINE LEAVES

Salmon: Rub the salmon with oil, then season with salt and pepper. Place a sprig of lemon thyme, and a strip of zest on each fillet. • If using fresh vine leaves, trim off the tough part of the stem. Blanch in boiling water for 3 minutes, then run under cold water and pat dry. If using preserved vine leaves, drain, rinse under water, and pat dry. • Lay out two vine leaves, overlapping them so that they are large enough to wrap a piece of salmon. Place a salmon fillet at one end and roll. Tie with a piece of water-soaked kitchen thread. Repeat with the remaining salmon and vine leaves. • Preheat a grill pan or barbecue over medium heat. Brush with oil. Place the salmon rolls on top and cook until tender, 8–12 minutes, turning once. Serve hot.

Sauce: While the salmon is cooking, combine the oil, lemon juice, capers, and parsley in a small bowl. Whisk lightly and serve with the salmon.

Salmon

- 4 salmon fillets, weighing about 6 ounces (180 g) each
- 1/4 cup (60 ml) extra-virgin olive oil
- Salt and freshly ground black pepper
- 4 sprigs lemon thyme
- 4 strips lemon zest
- 8 fresh or preserved grape vine leaves

Sauce

- 1/2 cup (125 ml) extra-virgin olive oil
- 2 tablespoons freshly squeezed lemon juice
- 2 teaspoons capers, finely chopped
- 1 tablespoon finely chopped fresh parsley

Serves: 4
Preparation: 20 minutes
Cooking: 12–15 minutes
Level: 2

FISH BAKED IN SALT WITH MEDITERRANEAN HERBS

Preheat the oven to 450°F (230°C/gas 8).
• Line a baking dish large enough to hold the whole fish and a thick layer of salt with aluminum foil. • Stuff the fish with a few sprigs of mint and fennel. • Cover the bottom of the pan with a thick layer of salt. Cover with mint, fennel, and pine needles, if using. • Place the fish on top and cover with the remaining herbs. • Cover with the remaining salt. The fish should be completely hidden beneath the salt. • Drizzle with the water and anisette. • Seal the baking dish with foil. • Bake for 45 minutes. • Remove the foil and bring to the table. Break the crust of salt in front of your guests and serve hot.

1	whole firm-fleshed fish, weighing about 3 pounds (1.5 kg), such as sea bass, red snapper, porgy, rockfish, tilefish, or grouper, gutted, with or without scales
1	bunch mint
1	bunch common or wild fennel leaves
8	pounds (4 kg) kosher salt or coarse sea salt
1	cup (250 g) pine needles (optional)
1/4	cup (60 ml) water
1	cup (250 ml) anisette

Serves: 4–6
Preparation: 15 minutes
Cooking: 45 minutes
Level: 2

■■■ *This is a classic Mediterranean dish. Don't worry about the fish becoming too salty; the salt forms a crust over the fish, keeping it moist and succulent but without making it overly salty.*

POULTRY

COQ AU VIN

Preheat the oven to 350°F (180°C/ gas 4). • Cut the chicken breasts into 2–3 pieces. Set aside. • Sauté the bacon in the butter and oil in a large frying pan over medium heat until it begins to brown, about 5 minutes. • Add the onions and sauté for 2 minutes. • Add the mushrooms and shallots and sauté for 5 minutes. • Use a slotted spoon to transfer the bacon and vegetables into a deep baking dish. • Dip the chicken in the seasoned flour. • Brown the chicken in the oil a few pieces at a time, then place in the dish. • Discard the oil in the pan. • Decrease the heat and pour in the brandy. Tilt the pan to ignite the brandy, then pour in the wine. Simmer, scraping up any brown bits. Add the sugar, then pour over the chicken. Season with salt and pepper. Add the thyme, bay leaves, and parsley. Sprinkle with the remaining seasoned flour. • Cover with aluminum foil and bake until the chicken is tender, about 40 minutes. • Sprinkle with the parsley and serve hot.

6	boneless skinless chicken breast halves
8	ounces (250 g) bacon, diced
2	tablespoons butter
1	tablespoon extra-virgin olive oil
12	pearl onions
4	ounces (125 g) button mushrooms, thinly sliced
6	shallots, thinly sliced
3	tablespoons all-purpose (plain) flour, seasoned with salt and freshly ground black pepper
2	tablespoons brandy
1¹/₂	cups (375 ml) dry red wine
1	teaspoon sugar
	Salt and freshly ground black pepper
1	sprig fresh thyme
2	bay leaves
2	tablespoons finely chopped fresh parsley

Serves: 4–6
Preparation: 20 minutes
Cooking: 50 minutes
Level: 2

CHICKEN NOISETTES WITH PESTO FILLING

Chicken Noisettes: Preheat the oven to 350°F (180°C/gas 4). • Trim each slice of bacon to the same size as the chicken breast halves. Reserve the trimmings. • Gently flatten the chicken with a meat tenderizer. Drizzle with the lemon juice and season with salt and pepper.

Pesto Filling: Combine all the filling ingredients and bacon trimmings in a food processor and process for 1 minute to make a paste. • Lay out the chicken breast halves. • Spread each breast with a quarter of the filling. Roll up the chicken. Wrap a bacon slice around each noisette, overlapping the ends. Insert a wooden skewer through the overlap and the center of each noisette. • Butter a baking dish. • Place the noisettes in the prepared dish and brush with melted butter. • Bake until golden brown and cooked through, about 30 minutes. • Slice each noisette and serve hot with vegetables.

Chicken Noisettes

4 slices bacon

4 boneless skinless chicken breast halves

1 tablespoon freshly squeezed lemon juice

Salt and freshly ground black pepper

2 tablespoons melted butter

Pesto Filling

1 cup (60 g) fresh bread crumbs

1 clove garlic

1/4 cup (45 g) pine nuts

1 tablespoon freshly squeezed lemon juice

1/4 cup (60 ml) extra-virgin olive oil

Salt and freshly ground black pepper

1 small bunch fresh parsley or basil

Seasonal vegetables, to serve

Serves: 4–6
Preparation: 20 minutes
Cooking: 30 minutes
Level: 2

CHICKEN WITH LEMON CAPER SAUCE

Dip the chicken in the seasoned flour until well coated. Shake off any excess. • Sauté the chicken in 2 tablespoons of butter in a large frying pan over medium heat until tender and golden, 6–8 minutes each side. • Transfer to serving dishes and keep warm. • Add the remaining 4 tablespoons of butter, capers, and lemon zest and juice to the pan. Simmer over low heat, stirring often, until thickened, about 5 minutes. • Season with salt and pepper. Spoon the sauce over the chicken. • Serve hot with seasonal vegetables on the side.

4   boneless skinless chicken breast halves

1   cup (150 g) all-purpose (plain) flour, seasoned with salt and freshly ground pepper

6   tablespoons (90 g) butter

1   tablespoon capers, drained

1   tablespoon finely grated lemon zest

5   tablespoons freshly squeezed lemon juice

Salt and freshly ground black pepper

Seasonal vegetables, to serve

Serves: 4
Preparation: 10 minutes
Cooking: 20 minutes
Level: 1

CHICKEN WITH PORCINI MUSHROOMS

Soak the porcini mushrooms in the boiling water in a small bowl for 30 minutes. • Drain, reserving the liquid. Coarsely chop the mushrooms. • Heat the oil in a large frying pan over medium-high heat. Add half the chicken and sauté until well browned. Remove and set aside. Repeat with the remaining chicken, adding a little more oil to the pan if needed. • Add the garlic and onion to the same pan. Sauté until softened, about 5 minutes. • Return all the chicken to the pan and add the mushrooms and their liquid. Add the tomatoes, chicken stock, potatoes, thyme, and oregano. Season with salt and pepper. Bring to a boil. • Decrease the heat and simmer until the chicken is tender, 40–50 minutes. • Serve hot.

3   ounces (90 g) dried porcini mushrooms

1/2 cup (125 ml) boiling water

1/4 cup (60 ml) extra-virgin olive oil

3   pounds (1.5 kg) chicken pieces

2   cloves garlic, finely chopped

1   onion, finely chopped

1   (14-ounce/400-g) can tomatoes, with juice

1/2 cup (125 ml) chicken stock (see Potato and Leek Soup, page 158)

1   pound (500 g) baby potatoes, halved

4   sprigs thyme, finely chopped

4   sprigs oregano, finely chopped

Salt and freshly ground black pepper

Serves: 4–6
Preparation: 20 minutes
    + 30 minutes to soak
Cooking: 1 hour
Level: 2

OVEN-BAKED PARMESAN CHICKEN

Preheat the oven to 425°F (220°C/gas 7).
• Mix the bread crumbs, Parmesan, scallions, lemon zest, and butter in a small bowl. Season with salt and pepper.
• Using a fork, press the mixture onto the chicken breasts to coat them evenly.
• Transfer to a roasting pan. • Bake until tender and cooked through, 20–30 minutes. • Remove the chicken from the pan and keep warm. • Add the lemon juice and parsley to the pan juices and mix well. Pour these juices over the chicken and serve hot with green beans.

1/2 cup (30 g) fresh white bread crumbs

3/4 cup (90 g) freshly grated Parmesan cheese

2 scallions (spring onions), finely chopped

Finely grated zest and freshly squeezed juice of 1/2 lemon

1/4 cup (60 g) butter, melted

Salt and freshly ground black pepper

4 boneless skinless chicken breast halves

2 tablespoons finely chopped fresh parsley

Green beans, to serve

Serves: 4
Preparation: 20 minutes
Cooking: 20–30 minutes
Level: 1

CHICKEN PROVENÇAL

Sauté the chicken in the oil in a large frying pan over medium-high heat until lightly browned, about 10 minutes.
• Season with salt and pepper. Remove the chicken from the pan and set aside.
• In the same pan, sauté the onion, garlic, and tomatoes until the tomatoes begin to break down, 8–10 minutes. Season with salt. • Lower the heat and pour in the wine. Stir in the rosemary, thyme, and olives. Simmer for 10 minutes. • Return the chicken to the pan.
• Cover and simmer over medium-low heat until the chicken is very tender, about 30 minutes. • Serve hot.

1 chicken, weighing about 3 pounds (1.5 kg), cut into 6–8 pieces

1/4 cup (60 ml) extra-virgin olive oil

Salt and freshly ground black pepper

1 onion, finely chopped

3 cloves garlic, finely chopped

6 firm-ripe tomatoes, peeled and coarsely chopped

2 cups (500 ml) dry white wine

1 tablespoon finely chopped fresh rosemary

1 tablespoon finely chopped fresh thyme

1 cup (100 g) black olives

Serves: 4
Preparation: 30 minutes
Cooking: 1 hour
Level: 1

SPANISH CHICKEN WITH CHORIZO

Sauté the chicken in 2 tablespoons of oil a large frying pan over medium heat until golden brown, about 10 minutes. Remove and set aside. Remove any fat from the pan. • Add the remaining 2 tablespoons of oil and sauté the onion, garlic, and bell peppers over medium heat until softened, about 5 minutes. • Return the chicken to the pan and add the paprika, sherry, tomatoes, bay leaf, and orange zest. Bring to a boil. • Cover and simmer, stirring occasionally, over low heat until chicken is tender, 35–40 minutes. • Add the chorizo and olives and simmer for 5 minutes. • Season with salt and pepper. • Serve hot.

■ ■ ■ *The Spanish chorizo used in this recipe is a dry cured sausage, quite unlike Mexican chorizo, which is a fresh sausage.*

8	chicken pieces such as thighs and drumsticks
1/4	cup (60 ml) extra-virgin olive oil
1	onion, thinly sliced
2	cloves garlic, finely chopped
1	red bell pepper (capsicum), seeded and thinly sliced
1	yellow bell pepper (capsicum), seeded and thinly sliced
2	teaspoons hot paprika
1/4	cup (60 ml) dry sherry or vermouth
1	(14-ounce/400-g) can tomatoes, with juice
1	bay leaf
1	strip orange zest
3	ounces (90 g) Spanish chorizo, thinly sliced
2/3	cup (60 g) pitted black olives
	Salt and freshly ground black pepper

Serves: 4
Preparation: 15 minutes
Cooking: 1 hour
Level: 1

CHICKEN STUFFED WITH MUSHROOMS AND TARRAGON

Preheat the oven to 400°F (200°C/ gas 6). • Sauté the leek, zucchini, garlic, and all the mushrooms in 2 tablespoons of oil in a large frying pan over medium heat until softened, about 5 minutes.
• Remove from the heat and stir in the tarragon. Season with pepper. • Gently flatten the chicken with a meat tenderizer. • Spread the stuffing evenly over each chicken breast. Roll up, folding in the ends, and secure with toothpicks. Brush with the remaining oil and place on a nonstick baking sheet. • Bake for 30–35 minutes, or until the juices run clear when pierced with a skewer.
• Remove the toothpicks and cut each roll into 1-inch (2.5-cm) slices.
• Serve hot with a green salad.

1	small leek, finely sliced
1	small zucchini (courgette), finely chopped
1	clove garlic, finely chopped
2	ounces (60 g) button mushrooms, finely chopped
2	ounces (60 g) oyster or shiitake mushrooms, finely chopped
3	tablespoons extra-virgin olive oil
2	tablespoons finely chopped fresh tarragon
	Freshly ground black pepper
4	boneless skinless chicken breast halves
	Green salad, to serve

Serves: 4
Preparation: 25 minutes
Cooking: 40 minutes
Level: 2

CHICKEN STUFFED WITH RICOTTA AND BELL PEPPERS

Heat a broiler (grill) to very hot and broil the bell pepper, turning often, until blackened all over. Place in a plastic bag and let rest for 10 minutes. • Pick all the blackened skin off the bell pepper and remove the seeds and pith from inside. Wipe clean with paper towels and chop into small pieces. • Mix the ricotta, arugula, pine nuts, and bell peppers in a small bowl. Season with salt and pepper. • Place 1–2 tablespoons of the mixture under the skin of each chicken breast. • Place the chicken breasts in a crock pot or slow cooker. Season with salt and pepper. Place a little butter on top of each breast and pour the stock around the chicken. Cook on the high setting for 2 hours. • Serve the chicken with the pan juices and arugula.

1	large red bell pepper (capsicum)
3/4	cup (200 g) fresh ricotta cheese
1	cup (50 g) arugula (rocket), chopped
1/4	cup (45 g) pine nuts, toasted
	Salt and freshly ground black pepper
4	boneless chicken breast halves, skin on, weighing about 6 ounces (180 g) each
2	tablespoons butter
1	cup (250 ml) chicken stock (see page 158)
	Arugula (rocket), to serve

Serves: 4
Preparation: 10 minutes
Cooking: 2 hours
Level: 2

■ ■ ■ *If short of time buy the grilled bell pepper ready to serve. Grilled peppers preserved in olive oil are available in most supermarkets. You will need about 3/4 cup (100 g).*

MOROCCAN LEMON CHICKEN KEBABS

Cut the chicken into 1-inch (2.5-cm) cubes. • Mix the parsley, rosemary, thyme, garlic, black pepper, lemon zest and juice, chile paste, and 2 tablespoons of oil in a medium bowl. • Add the chicken and toss well. • Marinate for at least 30 minutes. • Soak the bamboo skewers in cold water for 30 minutes. • Preheat a grill pan or barbecue on high. • Thread the chicken onto the skewers. • Cook on the grill, turning and brushing often with the remaining 2 tablespoons of oil, until tender and golden, about 10 minutes. • Serve hot with lemon wedges.

4	boneless skinless chicken breast halves
1	tablespoon finely chopped fresh parsley
1	tablespoon finely chopped fresh rosemary
2	teaspoons finely chopped fresh thyme
1	clove garlic, finely chopped
1	teaspoon crushed black peppercorns
	Finely grated zest and freshly squeezed juice of 1 lemon,
1	teaspoon red chile paste
1/4	cup (60 ml) extra-virgin olive oil
	Lemon wedges, to serve

■ ■ ■ *In Italy small hot chiles are coarsely chopped and preserved in jars with olive oil. The paste is very spicy. If you can't find Italian chile paste, use an Asian variety such as sambal olek, which is widely available in Asian markets and food stores.*

Serves: 6–8
Preparation: 10 minutes
 + 30 minutes to
 marinate
Cooking: 10 minutes
Level: 2

BUTTERFLIED QUAIL WITH LEMON AND SAGE

Preheat the oven to 350°F (180°C/gas 4).
• Mix 3 tablespoons of the oil, the lemon juice and zest, and garlic in a small bowl. Season with salt and pepper. Set aside.
• Heat the remaining 2 tablespoons of oil in a large frying pan over medium-high heat. Add the quail and chopped sage and sauté until well browned, about 10 minutes. • Transfer to a baking dish.
• Add the marinade and chicken stock to the pan. Return to the heat, bring to a boil, and simmer for 1 minute, stirring with a wooden spoon. • Pour the pan juices over the quail. • Bake until tender and cooked through, about 25 minutes.
• Garnish with whole sage leaves.
• Serve hot with arugula.

5	tablespoons extra-virgin olive oil
2	tablespoons freshly squeezed lemon juice
1/2	teaspoon finely grated lemon zest
1	clove garlic, finely chopped
	Salt and freshly ground black pepper
4	quails, butterflied
1	bunch sage leaves (1 tablespoon finely chopped, the rest to garnish
1/4	cup (60 ml) chicken stock (see Leek and Potato Soup, page 158)
	Arugula (rocket), to serve

Serves: 4
Preparation: 10 minutes
Cooking: 35 minutes
Level: 2

■ ■ ■ *To butterfly the quail, place on a cutting board breast side up and insert a knife into the cavity. Cut down through the backbone from neck to tail, then open the bird up and flatten with your hands. Cut off and discard the wing tips. If you can't find fresh quail, substitute with cornish hens.*

PANCETTA-WRAPPED QUAIL WITH WILD MUSHROOM STUFFING

Bring 2 cups (500 ml) of the chicken stock to a boil in a medium saucepan. • Sauté the leek and garlic in the oil in a large frying pan over medium heat until softened, about 5 minutes. • Add the rice and stir for 1 minute. • Add the mushrooms. Stir in 1/2 cup (125 ml) of wine and when this has been absorbed, begin stirring in the stock, 1/2 cup (125 ml) at a time. Cook and stir until each addition has been absorbed and the rice is tender, 15–18 minutes. • Season with salt and pepper. • Preheat the oven to 400°F (200°C/gas 6). • Fill each quail cavity with the mushroom mixture and secure with toothpicks. • Place all the quail in a roasting pan breast side up. Wrap a slice of pancetta around each quail, top with a sage leaf, and add 1/2 cup (125 ml) of the remaining stock and the remaining 1/2 cup (125 ml) wine to the pan. • Roast for 5 minutes, then lower the oven temperature to 350°F

3	cups (750 ml) chicken stock (see Leek and Potato Soup, page 158)
1	leek, finely sliced
1	clove garlic, finely chopped
2	tablespoons extra-virgin olive oil
1	cup (200 g) short-grain risotto rice
8	ounces (250 g) wild mushrooms
1	cup (250 ml) dry white wine
	Salt and freshly ground black pepper
4	quails or cornish hens
4	slices pancetta or bacon
8	sage leaves

Serves: 4
Preparation: 30 minutes
Cooking: 1 hour
Level: 3

(180°C/gas 4). Roast until tender, 20–25 minutes. Add more stock during cooking if the quails start to look dry. • Remove from the oven and keep warm. • Add the remaining 1/2 cup (125 ml) stock to the pan. Simmer over high heat for 5 minutes until the sauce has thickened, scraping any brown bits with a wooden spoon. • Serve the quail hot with the pan juices spooned over the top.

See photograph on the following page

GUINEA FOWL IN VINE LEAVES

Rinse out the guinea fowl and pat dry with paper towels. • Mix the honey, oil, orange juice, rosemary, and wine in a small bowl. • Place the guinea fowl in a large bowl and pour half the liquid over the top. Turn well to coat. Cover with aluminum foil and chill overnight, turning the bird over once or twice during the time. • Preheat the oven to 350°F (180°C/gas 4). • Wrap the guinea fowl in the leaves and secure with skewers. Place the bird in a large roasting pan. • Bake for 40 minutes. • Remove the vine leaves, reserving them, and bake for 20 minutes more. • Arrange the guinea fowl on the vine leaves. • Warm the remaining marinade in a small pan and pour over the guinea fowl. Serve hot.

2   **guinea fowl, cut in half**

3   **tablespoons honey**

3   **tablespoons extra-virgin olive oil**

3   **tablespoons freshly squeezed orange juice**

2   **teaspoons finely chopped fresh rosemary**

1/2   **cup (125 ml) dry white wine**

10   **preserved grape vine leaves**

Serves: 4
Preparation: 25 minutes + overnight to marinate
Cooking: 1 hour
Level: 2

■ ■ ■ *If you can't find guinea fowl substitute with lean young chicken.*

GUINEA FOWL BRAISED WITH VEGETABLES AND WINE

Rinse out the guinea fowl and pat dry with paper towels. • Brown the guinea fowl all over in the oil in a large pan over medium-high heat. • Remove from the pan and set aside. • In the same pan, sauté the bacon, garlic, and onions over medium heat until softened, about 5 minutes. • Return the birds to the pan. Add the carrots, wine, water, tomato paste, cloves, bay leaves, and cinnamon. Season with salt and pepper. Bring to a boil. • Cover and simmer over low heat for 30 minutes. Add a little water if needed during cooking. • Meanwhile, parboil the potatoes and carrots until almost tender, 5–10 minutes. Drain well. • Add the potatoes and carrots to the pan. Simmer for 15 minutes. The sauce should be reduced and slightly thickened. • Transfer the birds to serving platters and serve hot with the vegetables.

■ ■ ■ *If you can't find guinea fowl substitute with lean young chicken.*

2	guinea fowls
2	tablespoons extra-virgin olive oil
3	slices bacon, diced
2	cloves garlic, thinly sliced
1½	pounds (750 g) pearl onions
2	carrots, diced
½	cup (125 ml) dry white wine
1	cup (250 ml) water
1	tablespoon tomato paste (concentrate)
2	cloves
2	bay leaves
	2-inch (5-cm) long cinnamon stick
	Salt and freshly ground black pepper
1	pound (500 g) small potatoes, peeled
2	carrots, cut into chunks

Serves: 4
Preparation: 15 minutes
Cooking: 1 hour
Level: 2

ROAST GUINEA FOWL WITH ROSEMARY AND LEMON

Mix the oil, lemon juice, rosemary, and garlic in a small bowl. Season with salt and pepper. • Place the guinea fowl in a large bowl and pour in the marinade. Turn well to coat. Chill for 4 hours. • Preheat the oven to 350°F (180°C/gas 4). • Place the birds on a rack in a roasting pan. • Roast until tender and cooked through, 55–60 minutes. Baste every 15 minutes during roasting. • Serve hot with roast potatoes.

$1/4$ cup (60 ml) extra-virgin olive oil

2 tablespoons freshly squeezed lemon juice

1 tablespoon coarsely chopped fresh rosemary

1 clove garlic, finely chopped

Salt and freshly ground black pepper

2 guinea fowl, cut in half

Roasted potatoes, to serve

Serves: 4
Preparation: 10 minutes
 + 4 hours to marinate
Cooking: 1 hour
Level: 2

■ ■ ■ *If you can't find guinea fowl, substitute with lean young chicken.*
You can roast the potatoes under the rack in the same pan in which you roast the guinea fowl. They will take about 45 minutes to cook.

DUCK WITH OLIVES AND SHERRY

Preheat the oven to 350°F (180°C/gas 4).
• Soak the olives in warm water in a small bowl. • Season the duck inside and out with salt and pepper. • Truss the duck with kitchen string. Place in a roasting pan and prick all over with a fork. Roast for 1 hour. • Meanwhile, sauté the onion, carrots, and garlic in the oil in a casserole over medium heat until softened, about 5 minutes. • Carve the duck into pieces, discarding the backbone and rib cage. Transfer to the casserole. • Pour off the fat in the roasting pan and deglaze the pan with the chicken stock, scraping up any brown bits. Strain the liquid into the casserole. • Drain the olives and stir into the casserole with the wine, thyme, and parsley. Season with salt and pepper. Bring to a boil. Cover and bake in the oven until tender and cooked through, about 1 hour. • Serve hot.

1/2 cup (50 g) large green olives, pitted and sliced

1 (5-pound/2.5-kg) duck, as much fat removed as possible

Salt and freshly ground black pepper

1 medium onion, finely chopped

2 carrots, finely chopped

3 cloves garlic, finely chopped

1 tablespoon extra-virgin olive oil

3/4 cup (180 ml) chicken stock (see Leek and Potato Soup, page 158)

1/4 cup (60 ml) dry white wine or sherry

3/4 teaspoon dried thyme

1 tablespoon finely chopped fresh parsley

Serves: 4
Preparation: 30 minutes
Cooking: 2 hours
Level: 3

CHICKEN, OLIVE, AND ONION CASSEROLE

Mix the chicken with the wine, oregano, and bay leaves in a large bowl. Cover with aluminum foil and chill overnight. • Drain the chicken, reserving the marinade. • Preheat the oven to 350°F (180°C/gas 4). • Heat the oil in a large frying pan over medium-high heat. Add the chicken a few pieces at a time and brown well, 8–10 minutes. • Transfer to a baking dish. • In the same pan, sauté the onions and garlic over medium heat until softened, about 5 minutes. • Add the paprika and cook, stirring, for 2 minutes. • Pour in the chicken stock and reserved marinade. Bring to a boil. • Pour the onion mixture over the chicken and add the olives. Season with salt and pepper. • Cover with aluminum foil and bake until the chicken is tender, about 1 hour. • Serve hot with freshly baked bread.

■ ■ ■ *Traditionally this recipe is made with rabbit, but it works equally well with chicken.*

2	pounds (1 kg) chicken (or rabbit), cleaned and cut into pieces
1½	cups (375 ml) dry white wine
3	sprigs fresh oregano
3	bay leaves
⅓	cup (90 ml) extra-virgin olive oil
8	ounces (250 g) pearl onions, halved
6	cloves garlic, unpeeled
1	tablespoon sweet paprika
¾	cup (180 ml) chicken stock (see Leek and Potato Soup, page 158)
½	cup (50 g) black olives
	Salt and freshly ground black pepper
	Crusty bread, to serve

Serves: 4
Preparation: 15 minutes + overnight to marinate
Cooking: 1½ hours
Level: 2

CHICKEN WITH ROASTED GARLIC

Preheat the oven to 400°F (200°C/ gas 6). • Place the garlic bulbs on a baking sheet lined with aluminum foil and drizzle with a little oil. Wrap and seal. Roast for 1 hour. Set aside. • Mix the lemon and orange zest and juice, wine, rosemary, chopped garlic, salt, pepper, and chicken in a large bowl. Marinate in the refrigerator for 2 hours. • Drain the chicken, reserving the marinade. • Heat the oil in a large frying pan over medium-high heat. Add the chicken a few pieces and brown well, 8–10 minutes. • Add the reserved marinade. Cover and simmer over low heat until tender, 25–30 minutes. • Remove the chicken from the pan. Set aside and keep warm. • Strain the cooking liquid. Serve the chicken and roasted garlic with the sauce.

4	garlic bulbs + 2 cloves, finely chopped
	Finely grated zest and freshly squeezed juice of 1 lemon
	Finely grated zest and freshly squeezed juice of 1 orange
2	cups (500 ml) dry white wine
1	sprig rosemary
1	teaspoon salt
$1/2$	teaspoon freshly ground black pepper
1	chicken (or rabbit), cut into 8 pieces
2	tablespoons extra-virgin olive oil

Serves: 4
Preparation: 40 minutes + 2 hours to marinate
Cooking: 1 hour 30 minutes
Level: 3

■ ■ ■ *Traditionally this recipe is made with rabbit, but it works equally well with chicken.*

CHICKEN, BELL PEPPER, OLIVE, AND FETA PIE

Heat a broiler (grill) to very hot and broil the bell pepper, turning often, until blackened all over. Place in a plastic bag and let rest for 10 minutes. • Pick all the blackened skin off the bell pepper and remove the seeds and pith from inside. Wipe clean with paper towels and chop into small pieces. • Preheat the oven to 350°F (180°C/gas 4). • Sauté the leek and garlic in 1 tablespoon of oil in a large frying pan over medium heat until softened, about 5 minutes. Set aside. • Heat the remaining 1 tablespoon of oil in the same pan over medium heat. Brown the chicken, 6–8 minutes each batch. • Cook the spinach in a little salted water until just tender, 2–3 minutes. Drain well, squeezing out any excess moisture. Chop coarsely. • Mix the chicken, spinach, bell peppers, olives, feta, parsley, oregano, eggs, and cream in

2	red bell peppers (capsicums)
1	large leek, thinly sliced
1	clove garlic, finely chopped
2	tablespoons extra-virgin olive oil
6	boneless skinless chicken breast halves, diced
1	bunch baby spinach leaves
1/2	cup (50 g) black olives, pitted and cut in half
6	ounces (180 g) feta cheese, crumbled
2	tablespoons finely chopped fresh parsley
1	tablespoon finely chopped fresh oregano
3	large eggs
1/4	cup (60 ml) heavy (double) cream
	Freshly ground black pepper

8 sheets phyllo pastry
$1/3$ cup (90 g) melted
  butter

Serves: 4–6
Preparation: 50 minutes
Cooking: 65–75 minutes
Level: 3

a large bowl. Season with pepper. Set aside. • Butter a 9-inch (23-cm) square baking dish. • Lay out two sheets of phyllo pastry on a work surface and brush lightly with butter. • Place another two sheets on top and brush again with butter. Repeat until you have four double sheets. • Line the baking dish with the phyllo pastry, trimming the edges to fit. • Fill with the chicken mixture. • Brush the remaining sheets with butter. Place the phyllo pastry on top of the baking dish, tucking the edges inside. • Brush the top with butter. • Bake until golden brown, 40–45 minutes. • Serve hot.

See photograph on the following page

VEAL, BEEF, PORK AND LAMB

VEAL SALTIMBOCCA

Lightly pound the veal with a meat tenderizer so that it is thin and of even thickness. • Melt the butter in a large frying pan over high heat. Cook the veal until browned, 2–3 minutes on each side. If the scallops don't all fit in the pan in a single layer, cook them in two pans or in two batches. • Remove from the pan, top each scallop with a half slice of prosciutto and two sage leaves. Secure with toothpicks. • Return the veal to the pan with the butter and add the chopped sage. Cook over medium heat for 1 minute. Season with salt. • Turn up the heat. Pour in the wine and let it evaporate. • Discard the toothpicks and serve at once.

1 pound (500 g) veal scallops (escalopes)

1/4 cup (60 g) butter, cut up

8 slices prosciutto (Parma ham)

Bunch of fresh sage + 1 tablespoon coarsely chopped fresh sage

Salt

1/2 cup (125 ml) dry white wine

Serves: 4
Preparation: 8 minutes
Cooking: 10 minutes
Level: 2

VEAL WITH MOZZARELLA, EGGPLANT, AND TOMATOES

Lightly pound the veal with a meat tenderizer so that it is thin and of even thickness. • Heat the butter and 3 tablespoons of oil in a large frying pan over high heat. Cook the veal until browned, 2–3 minutes on each side. If the scallops don't all fit in the pan in a single layer, cook them in two pans or in two batches. • Preheat the broiler (grill).

• Place two slices of mozzarella on top of each piece of veal. • Broil (grill) the veal until the cheese has melted, about 2 minutes. • Meanwhile, broil the tomatoes until just softened, about 5 minutes.

• Place a grill pan over medium-high heat.

• Brush the eggplant with the remaining 2 tablespoons of oil and until tender, about 3 minutes each side. Remove from the heat and set aside. • Cut each veal scallop in half and top with 2 slices of eggplant and half a tomato. • Heat the remaining pan juices with the stock and thyme. Bring to a boil and simmer for 2 minutes. • Pour the pan juices over the veal and serve hot.

1	pound (500 g) veal scallops (escalopes)
2	tablespoons butter
5	tablespoons extra-virgin olive oil
8	ounces (250 g) mozzarella cheese, thinly sliced
4	tomatoes, cut in half
1	large eggplant (aubergine), thinly sliced
1	cup (250 ml) beef stock (see Easy French Onion Soup, page 150)
4	sprigs fresh thyme

Serves: 4
Preparation: 15 minutes
Cooking: 20 minutes
Level: 2

VEAL WITH BALSAMIC VINEGAR

Lightly pound the veal with a meat tenderizer so that it is thin and of even thickness. • Season the veal with salt and pepper. • Heat the oil in a large frying pan over high heat. Cook the veal until browned, 2–3 minutes on each side. If the scallops don't all fit in the pan in a single layer, cook them in two batches. • With all the veal in the pan, and add the balsamic vinegar and let it evaporate. • Add the arugula and let it wilt for 1 minute. • Remove from the heat and let rest for 3 minutes. • Sprinkle with the Parmesan and season with salt and pepper. • Serve hot.

$1^1/_2$ pounds (750 g) veal scallops (escalopes)

Salt and freshly ground black pepper

2 tablespoons extra-virgin olive oil

3 tablespoons balsamic vinegar

2 cups (100 g) arugula (rocket), coarsely chopped

5 ounces (150 g) Parmesan cheese, shaved

Serves: 6
Preparation: 10 minutes
Cooking: 10 minutes
Level: 1

VEAL SHANKS

Dip the veal shanks in the seasoned flour until well coated, shaking off the excess. • Heat the oil in a large frying pan over medium heat. • Brown the veal for 2 minutes on each side. • Remove from the pan and keep warm. • Add the garlic, onion, carrot, and celery to the pan. Sauté until softened, about 5 minutes. • Turn up the heat. Pour in the wine and let it evaporate. • Stir in the tomatoes, beef stock, and tomato paste and return the veal to the pan. • Bring to a boil. Add the basil and parsley. Season with salt and pepper. Decrease the heat, cover, and simmer until the meat starts to come away from the bone, about 2 hours. • Serve hot.

4	veal shanks
2	tablespoons all-purpose (plain) flour, seasoned with salt and pepper
2	tablespoons extra-virgin olive oil
1	clove garlic, chopped
1	onion, chopped
1	carrot, diced
2	stalks celery, diced
1/2	cup (125 ml) dry white wine
4	tomatoes, chopped
1	cup (250 ml) beef stock (see Easy French Onion Soup, page 150)
2	tablespoons tomato paste
1	tablespoon torn fresh basil
1	tablespoon finely chopped fresh parsley
	Salt and freshly ground black pepper

Serves: 4
Preparation: 15 minutes
Cooking: 2 hours
Level: 1

VEAL WITH TUNA SAUCE

Veal: Pour the wine into a large bowl, reserving 1/2 cup (125 ml). • Add the carrot, cloves, and bay leaves. Season with salt and pepper and add the veal. Cover and let marinate in the refrigerator for 1 day, turning occasionally.

Tuna Sauce: Place the mayonnaise, tuna, lemon juice, capers, and reserved 1/2 cup (125 ml) of wine in a food processor and process until smooth. • Transfer to a small bowl and set aside. • Remove the veal from the marinade and wrap it in a piece of cheesecloth. Secure the cheesecloth, tying the ends with kitchen string. • Place in a large saucepan over medium heat. Add the marinade and 1 cup (250 ml) of beef stock and simmer until tender, about 2 hours, adding more beef stock if the pan dries out. • Remove the veal from the pan and transfer to a chopping board. Remove the muslin and slice the meat thinly. Let cool completely. • Arrange the veal on a serving dish with the tuna sauce. • Serve at room temperature.

Veal

3	cups (750 ml) very dry white wine
1	carrot, finely chopped
3	cloves
2	bay leaves
	Salt and freshly ground black pepper
2	pounds (1 kg) lean boned veal roast

Tuna Sauce

1/2	cup (125 ml) mayonnaise
2	cups (250 g) canned tuna, drained and crumbled
3	tablespoons freshly squeezed lemon juice
1	tablespoon salt-cured capers, rinsed
1–2	cups (250–500 ml) beef stock (see Easy French Onion Soup, page 150)

Serves: 6–8
Preparation: 25 minutes
  + 1 day to marinate
Cooking: 2 hours
Level: 2

FRIED VEAL CHOPS, MILANESE-STYLE

Lightly pound the veal with a meat tenderizer so that it is of even thickness. • Dip the veal in the eggs and then in the bread crumbs. Press down well so that the bread crumbs stick all over. • Heat the butter and oil in a large frying pan over medium heat. • Add the veal chops and fry until a thick golden crust forms, 2–3 minutes. Turn and cook in the same way on the other side. If the chops don't all fit in the pan in a single layer, cook them in two pans or in two batches. • Drain well on paper towels and season with salt. • Garnish with the lemon wedges and serve hot.

4   **large veal chops, bone-in**
2   **large eggs, lightly beaten**
$1^1/2$ **cups (200 g) fine dry bread crumbs**
$1/2$ **cup (125 g) butter**
1   **tablespoon extra-virgin olive oil**
   Salt
   Lemon wedges, to garnish

Serves: 4
Preparation: 10 minutes
Cooking: 10 minutes
Level: 1

■■■ *This is a classic Milanese dish. It is very popular all over Italy and can be ordered by simply asking for "una milanese."*

STEAK SALAD

Season the steak generously with salt and pepper. • Place a grill pan over medium-high heat. • Add 2 tablespoons of oil and cook the steaks for 8–15 minutes, depending on how well done you like your steak. • Arrange the arugula and tomatoes on serving plates. • Slice the steaks and place on top of the salad. • Drizzle with the remaining 4 tablespoons of oil and the balsamic vinegar. Season with salt and pepper and serve hot.

2   pounds (1 kg) tenderloin steak

Salt and freshly ground black pepper

1/4 cup (60 ml) + 2 tablespoons extra-virgin olive oil

1   bunch fresh arugula (rocket) or other tender salad greens

20 cherry tomatoes, halved

1/4 cup (60 ml) balsamic vinegar

Serves: 4
Preparation: 10 minutes
Cooking: 8–15 minutes
Level: 1

■■■ *There are many slight variations on this dish which has become a modern classic in restaurants all over Italy. Vary the cooking time of the steak so that it is cooked rare, medium, or well done to your liking.*

BEEF CARPACCIO

Wrap the beef tightly in plastic wrap (cling film) and freeze until firm, about 2 hours. • Use a very sharp knife to cut the beef very thinly into 1/8-inch (3-mm) slices. • Dress the arugula with the balsamic vinegar and oil. • Lay the beef slices in a circle, slightly overlapping and top with the arugula and shavings of cheese. Season with salt and pepper. • Serve at room temperature.

1	pound (500 g) very fresh beef fillet
2	cups (100 g) arugula (rocket)
1	tablespoon balsamic vinegar
3	tablespoons extra-virgin olive oil
2	ounces (60 g) Parmesan or pecorino cheese, shaved
	Salt and freshly ground black pepper

Serves: 6
Preparation: 10 minutes
  + 2 hours to freeze
Level: 1

PORK CUTLETS
WITH PROSCIUTTO

Dip the chops in the seasoned flour until well coated, shaking off the excess. Dip in the egg and then in the bread crumbs. Press down well so that the bread crumbs stick all over. • Heat the butter and oil in a large frying pan over medium heat. • Add the chops and fry until cooked through and a thick golden crust forms, about 5 minutes on each side. • Drain well on paper towels. • Preheat the broiler (grill). • Place the chops on a baking sheet. Top each one with a slice of prosciutto, shavings of Parmesan, and 1 tablespoon of cream. • Broil the chops until the cheese has melted, about 2 minutes. • Serve hot.

4	pork loin chops, bone-in
1	cup (150 g) all-purpose (plain) flour, seasoned with salt and freshly ground black pepper
1	large egg, lightly beaten
1	cup (150 g) fine dry bread crumbs
3	tablespoons butter
1	tablespoon extra-virgin olive oil
4	slices prosciutto (Parma ham)
2	ounces (60 g) Parmesan cheese, shaved
1/4	cup (60 ml) light (single) cream

Serves: 4
Preparation: 10 minutes
Cooking: 15 minutes
Level: 1

PORK CHOPS WITH GREMOLATA

Pork Chops: Preheat the oven to 400°F (200°C/gas 6). • Put the tomatoes on a baking tray and drizzle with 1 tablespoon of oil. Roast for 10 minutes. • Sprinkle the tomatoes with the chives. Set aside and keep warm. • Heat 1 tablespoon of oil in a large frying pan over high heat. • Add the chops and sear for 1 minute on each side. • Transfer to a baking dish. • Mix the remaining 2 tablespoons of oil, lemon zest and juice, mustard, and honey in a small bowl. Drizzle over the chops and season with salt and pepper. • Bake until cooked through, 10–15 minutes. Let rest for 5 minutes.

Gremolata: Mix the lemon zest, parsley, and garlic in a small bowl.
• Sprinkle the gremolata over the chops. Serve hot with the roasted tomatoes on the side.

Pork Chops

8	ounces (250 g) cherry tomatoes
1/4	cup (60 ml) extra-virgin olive oil
1	small bunch chives, finely chopped
4	pork loin chops, bone-in
	Finely grated zest and freshly squeezed juice of 1 lemon
1	tablespoon Dijon mustard
1	teaspoon honey
	Salt and freshly ground black pepper

Gremolata

	Finely grated zest of 2 lemons
1/4	cup finely chopped fresh parsley
2	cloves garlic, finely chopped

Serves: 4
Preparation: 20 minutes
Cooking: 20–25 minutes
Level: 1

PORK CHOPS WITH QUINCE

Heat the oil in a large frying pan over high heat. • Add the chops and sear for 2 minutes on each side. Set aside. • Sauté the onion and garlic in the remaining oil in a large frying pan over medium heat until softened, about 5 minutes. • Add the quince and simmer for 3 minutes. • Turn up the heat. Pour in the wine and let it evaporate. • Stir in the orange juice, chicken stock, cinnamon stick, and honey. Simmer over low heat until the sauce has thickened slightly, about 10 minutes. • Return the pork to the pan and simmer until cooked through, about 10 minutes. • Stir in the parsley. Season with salt and pepper. • Serve hot.

1	tablespoon extra-virgin olive oil
4	pork loin chops, bone-in
1	medium onion, thinly sliced
1	clove garlic, finely chopped
2	tablespoons extra-virgin olive oil
1	medium quince, peeled, cored, and cut into thin wedges
1/2	cup (125 ml) dry white wine
	Freshly squeezed juice of 1 orange
1/3	cup (90 ml) chicken stock (see Leek and Potato Soup, page 158)
	2-inch (5-cm) long cinnamon stick
1	tablespoon honey
1	tablespoon finely chopped fresh parsley
	Salt and freshly ground black pepper

Serves: 4
Preparation: 20 minutes
Cooking: 40 minutes
Level: 2

PORK CHOPS WITH HONEY MUSTARD SAUCE

Preheat the oven to 350°F (180°C/gas 4).
• Mix the bread crumbs, butter, garlic, oregano, basil, and parsley in a small bowl. Season with salt and pepper.
• Dip the chops in the egg and then in the bread crumb mixture. Press down well so that the bread crumbs stick all over. • Cook the pears in 1 tablespoon of butter and 1 tablespoon of honey in a large frying pan, turning often, until the pears turn golden and caramelize. Set aside. • Melt the remaining 1 tablespoon of butter and oil in a large frying pan over medium heat. • Add the chops and fry until tender and cooked through, about 5 minutes each side. • Cook the mustard, the remaining honey, and chicken stock in a small saucepan over medium-high heat until thick. • Serve the chops hot with the pears and sauce.

2 cups (120 g) fresh white bread crumbs

1/4 cup (60 g) butter, melted

1 teaspoon finely chopped garlic

2 teaspoons finely chopped fresh oregano

2 teaspoons torn fresh basil

2 teaspoons finely chopped fresh parsley

Salt and freshly ground black pepper

4 pork loin chops, bone-in

1 large egg, beaten

3 pears, cored and cut into quarters

2 tablespoons butter

2 tablespoons honey

1 tablespoon extra-virgin olive oil

1 tablespoon mustard

3/4 cup (180 ml) chicken stock (see Leek and Potato Soup, page 158)

Serves: 4
Preparation: 20 minutes
Cooking: 25 minutes
Level: 2

PORK IN WALNUT SAUCE

Season the pork with salt and let rest in the refrigerator for 1 hour. • Preheat the oven to 400°F (200°C/gas 6). • Rub the pork with butter and season with nutmeg and pepper. • Heat a large frying pan over high heat. • Brown the pork on all sides. • Add the brandy, tilting the pan to ignite it. Let it burn out. • Transfer the pork onto a low rack (or an upturned plate) in a fairly deep baking dish that will hold it snugly. Cover with the milk and bake until tender 1 1/2–2 hours. (You can also cook it on the top of the stove over low heat if you prefer.) After about 1 hour, add the walnuts. Season with salt and pepper. Add more milk to keep the meat moist. • Remove the pork from the pan and slice it thinly. • Serve the pork with baked apples and mashed potato, drizzled with the sauce.

3	pounds (1.5 kg) pork tenderloin
	Salt and freshly ground black pepper
1	tablespoon butter
	Freshly grated nutmeg
1	tablespoon brandy
4	cups (1 liter) milk + more if needed
5	ounces (150 g) walnuts
	Mashed potato, to serve

Serves: 6–8
Preparation: 15 minutes + 1 hour to rest
Cooking: 1 1/2–2 hours
Level: 2

PORK APPLE ROLLS

Preheat the oven to 350°F (180°C/gas 4). • Mix the apples, golden raisins, and lemon juice in a small bowl. • Spread each pork slice with the plum sauce to within 1 inch (2.5 cm) of the edges. Place a small amount of the apple mixture in the center. Roll up and tie with kitchen string. • Place the pork rolls in a baking dish seam-side down. • Mix the apple juice, soy sauce, and honey in a small bowl and pour it over the pork. Cover with aluminum foil. • Bake until tender, 20–25 minutes. • Serve hot with steamed snow peas.

2　apples, peeled, cored, and coarsely chopped

1/2　cup (60 g) golden raisins (sultanas)

Freshly squeezed juice of 1/2 lemon

2　pounds (1 kg) pork tenderloin, cut in 1/4-inch (5-mm) thick slices

1/2　cup (125 ml) plum sauce

1/2　cup (125 ml) apple juice

1　tablespoon light soy sauce

1　tablespoon honey

Snow peas (mangetout), to serve

Serves: 6–8
Preparation: 20 minutes
Cooking: 20–25 minutes
Level: 2

PORK MEDALLIONS WITH WINTER FRUITS

Combine the apple, pear, wine, and chicken stock in a large saucepan. Bring to a boil. • Simmer over low heat until the fruit has softened slightly, about 10 minutes. • Add the dried fruit and cinnamon. Cook for about 30 minutes until the fruit is plump. • Remove from the heat and let cool. • Heat the oil in a large frying pan over medium heat. • Add the pork and fry until browned, about 2 minutes on each side. Remove from the pan and set aside. • Turn up the heat. Add the brandy and let it evaporate. • Add a little of the cooking liquid from the fruit. Cook over medium heat, stirring constantly, to deglaze the pan. • Stir in the fruit mixture and cook until heated through, about 2 minutes. • Return the pork to the pan. Cook, stirring occasionally, until tender and cooked through, about 5 minutes. • Serve hot.

1   apple, peeled, cored, and diced

1   pear, peeled, cored, and diced

1/2 cup (125 ml) dry white wine

1/2 cup (125 ml) chicken stock (see Leek and Potato Soup, page 158)

3   ounces (90 g) dried fruit such as apricots, peaches, pears, and prunes

1   teaspoon ground cinnamon

1   tablespoon extra-virgin olive oil

1   pound (500 g) pork tenderloin, cut into 1/4-inch (5-mm) thick medallions

2   tablespoons brandy

Serves: 4
Preparation: 20 minutes
Cooking: 50 minutes
Level: 2

PORK MEDALLIONS WITH ORANGE SALSA

Orange Salsa: Cut a few strips of zest from the orange and reserve. Slice the top and bottom off the orange, then cut off the zest and pith, following the curve of the fruit. Cut between the membranes to release the segments, catching any juices in a bowl.
• Mix the orange segments, juice, and scallion in a small bowl. Season with salt and pepper. Set aside.

Medallions: Lightly pound the pork with a meat tenderizer so that it is thin and of even thickness. • Mix the bread crumbs, Parmesan, and oregano in a small bowl. Season with salt and pepper. • Dip the pork in the egg and then in the bread crumbs. Press down well so that the bread crumbs stick all over. • Heat the oil in a large frying pan over medium heat. • Add the pork and fry until cooked through and lightly browned, 4–5 minutes each side. • Drain on paper towels. • Serve hot with the orange salsa on top.

Orange Salsa

1   large orange
1   scallion (spring onion), finely chopped
    Salt and freshly ground black pepper

Medallions

4   pork scallops
2   cups (120 g) fresh white bread crumbs
1/2 cup (60 g) freshly grated Parmesan cheese
1   teaspoon dried oregano
    Salt and freshly ground black pepper
1   large egg, lightly beaten
2   tablespoons extra-virgin olive oil

Serves: 4
Preparation: 30 minutes
Cooking: 10 minutes
Level: 2

LAMB STEW WITH BUTTER BEANS, OLIVES, AND ORZO

Brown the lamb shanks with the garlic and onion in the oil in a large saucepan over medium heat for 5 minutes. • Add the beef stock, sprigs of oregano, tomato paste, and 1 cup (250 ml) of water. Bring to a boil. • Decrease the heat, cover, and simmer until tender and cooked through, about 40 minutes. • Remove the shanks from the pan and slice the meat off the bone. Set aside. • Add the pasta and the remaining 1 cup (250 ml) water. • Cook the pasta until al dente, about 5 minutes. • Add the butter beans, olives, lamb, and oregano. Season with salt and pepper. Cook for 5 minutes. • Serve hot.

4	lamb shanks
2	cloves garlic, finely chopped
1	onion, finely chopped
2	tablespoons extra-virgin olive oil
2	cups (500 ml) beef stock (see easy French Onion soup, page 150)
4	sprigs fresh oregano
2	tablespoons tomato paste (concentrate)
2	cups (500 ml) water
4	ounces (125 g) orzo (risoni)
1	cup (200 g) canned butter beans or lima beans, drained
1/2	cup (50 g) black olives
2	teaspoons finely chopped fresh oregano
	Salt and freshly ground black pepper

Serves: 4
Preparation: 15 minutes
Cooking: 55 minutes
Level: 2

VEGETABLES AND SALADS

MOROCCAN BEANS

Sauté the ginger, cinnamon, cumin seeds, and turmeric in the oil in a large saucepan over medium heat for 1 minute. • Add the onions and sauté until softened, about 5 minutes. • Stir in the red kidney beans, butter beans, garbanzo beans, tomatoes, and vegetable stock and bring to a boil. Decrease the heat and simmer for 10 minutes. • Toast the pine nuts in a small pan over medium heat until golden, 5 minutes. • Add the currants and pine nuts to the beans. Sprinkle with the basil and serve hot.

1 tablespoon finely grated ginger

1 teaspoon ground cinnamon

1 teaspoon cumin seeds

1/4 teaspoon turmeric

2 tablespoons extra-virgin olive oil

2 onions, chopped

1 (14-ounce/400-g) can red kidney beans, drained

1 (14-ounce/400-g) can butter beans or lima beans, drained

1 (14-ounce/400-g) can garbanzo beans (chickpeas), drained

1 (14-ounce/400-g) can tomatoes, with juice

1 cup (250 ml) vegetable stock (see page 251)

1/3 cup (60 g) pine nuts

1/3 cup (60 g) currants

Fresh basil leaves, torn, to garnish

Serves: 6
Preparation: 5 minutes
Cooking: 25 minutes
Level: 1

SPINACH WITH RAISINS AND PINE NUTS

Soak the raisins in cold water for 15 minutes. Drain well. • Cook the spinach in a little lightly salted water until wilted, 5–7 minutes. • Drain and chop coarsely. • Toast the pine nuts in a large frying pan over medium heat until golden, about 5 minutes. Remove from the pan and set aside. • Add the oil to the same pan. Add the onion and garlic and sauté over medium heat until softened, about 5 minutes. • Add the spinach and raisins. Season with salt and pepper and toss gently. Sprinkle with the pine nuts. • Serve hot.

3 tablespoons golden raisins (sultanas)

2 pounds (1 kg) spinach, tough stems removed

2 tablespoons pine nuts

3 tablespoons extra-virgin olive oil

1 medium onion, finely chopped

1 clove garlic, finely chopped

Salt and freshly ground black pepper

Serves: 6–8
Preparation: 20 minutes + 15 minutes to soak
Cooking: 10–15 minutes
Level: 1

MODERN POTATO DAUPHINOISE

Preheat the oven to 400°F (200°C/gas 6).
• Line a large baking dish with aluminum
foil and butter the foil. • Sauté the leeks,
shallots, and thyme in the oil in a large
frying pan over medium heat until golden
and softened, about 5 minutes. • Add the
parsley. Season with salt and pepper. Set
aside. • Peel the sweet and white potatoes
and cut into 1/4-inch (5-mm) slices. Layer
half the white potato slices over the
bottom of the prepared pan. Spread a
little pesto over the slices. • Spread evenly
with one-third of the leek mixture. Top
with a layer of sweet potato slices, a thin
layer of pesto and another third of the leek
mixture. Continue layering the potatoes,
pesto, and leek mixture until all the
ingredients have been used, finishing with
a layer of sweet potatoes. • Pour the
cream over the top and sprinkle with the
Parmesan and paprika. • Bake until the
potatoes are tender, about 50 minutes.
• Serve warm.

3 **large leeks,
   thinly sliced**

6 **shallots,
   finely chopped**

1 **tablespoon finely
   chopped fresh
   thyme**

2 **tablespoons extra-
   virgin olive oil**

3 **tablespoons finely
   chopped fresh
   parsley**

   **Salt and freshly
   ground black pepper**

1 1/2 **pounds (750 g)
   sweet potatoes**

1 1/2 **pounds (750 g)
   white potatoes**

   **Pesto (see
   Vegetable Lasagna
   Stacks with Pesto,
   page 226)**

1/2 **cup (125 ml) light
   (single) cream**

1/2 **cup (60 g) freshly
   grated Parmesan**

1/2 **teaspoon sweet
   paprika**

**Serves: 6–8
Preparation: 35 minutes
Cooking: 55 minutes
Level: 2**

ZUCCHINI MOUSSAKA

Preheat the oven to 350°F (180°C/gas 4). • Butter a large baking dish or 4–6 individual baking dishes. • Fry the zucchini in batches in the oil in a large, deep frying pan until lightly browned, 5–7 minutes per batch. Drain on paper towels. • Add the onion, bell peppers, and garlic to the same pan. Sauté over medium heat until the onions have softened, about 5 minutes. • Stir in the tomatoes, tomato paste, and mint. Simmer for 2 minutes. • Layer half the zucchini slices in the prepared dish with half the tomato sauce. Sprinkle with the Gruyère. Top with the remaining tomato sauce, and finish with a layer of zucchini slices. • Whisk the flour, yogurt, and eggs in a medium bowl. Pour over the zucchini. Sprinkle with the Parmesan. • Bake for 30–40 minutes, until bubbling and browned. • Serve hot.

5	zucchini (courgettes), sliced thinly lengthwise
1/3	cup (90 ml) extra-virgin olive oil
1	onion, chopped
2	red bell peppers (capsicums), seeded, cored, and thinly sliced
1	clove garlic, finely chopped
1	(14-ounce/400-g) can tomatoes, with juice
2	tablespoons tomato paste (concentrate)
2	tablespoons finely chopped fresh mint
5	ounces (150 g) Gruyère, thinly sliced
1/3	cup (50 g) all-purpose (plain) flour
2	cups (500 ml) plain yogurt
2	large eggs
1 1/2	cups (185 g) freshly grated Parmesan

Serves: 4–6
Preparation: 20 minutes
Cooking: 50 minutes
Level: 2

STUFFED BELL PEPPERS

Preheat the oven to 400°F (200°C/ gas 6). • Place the bell peppers skin-side down in a large roasting pan. • Bake for 5 minutes. • Meanwhile, mix the capers, garlic, bread crumbs, parsley, golden raisins, pine nuts, and oil in a medium bowl. Season with salt and pepper. • Spoon the mixture into the cavities of the partly cooked bell peppers. • Bake until the filling is browned and the bell peppers are softened enough to eat, 10–15 minutes. • Serve warm.

4   yellow bell peppers (capsicums), cut in half lengthwise, seeded, and cored

2   tablespoons salt-cured capers, rinsed and finely chopped

2   cloves garlic, finely chopped

1/2   cup (75 g) fine dry bread crumbs

2   tablespoons finely chopped fresh parsley

2   tablespoons golden raisins (sultanas), soaked in warm water for 1 hour and drained

2   tablespoons pine nuts

1/2   cup (125 ml) extra-virgin olive oil

  Salt and freshly ground black pepper

Serves: 4
Preparation: 10 minutes
Cooking: 15–20 minutes
Level: 1

RATATOUILLE

Sauté the onions in the oil in a large saucepan over medium heat until softened, about 5 minutes. • Stir in the eggplants and zucchini, followed by the bell peppers, tomatoes, bay leaf, thyme, and garlic. Season with salt and pepper. • Cover and simmer over low heat for 50 minutes. • Stir in the olives and garnish with the basil. • Serve hot.

2	onions, chopped
1/2	cup (125 ml) extra-virgin olive oil
1	pound (500 g) eggplant (aubergine), diced
1	pound (500 g) zucchini (courgettes), diced
1	red or yellow bell pepper (capsicum), seeded, cored, and cut into thin strips
1	green bell pepper (capsicum), seeded, cored, and cut into thin strips
2	pounds (1 kg) tomatoes, peeled, seeded, and chopped
1	bay leaf
1	tablespoon finely chopped fresh thyme
2	cloves garlic, finely chopped
	Salt and freshly ground black pepper
1/2	cup (50 g) black olives
	Fresh basil, torn

Serves: 6
Preparation: 25 minutes
Cooking: 1 hour
Level: 1

BELL PEPPER STEW

Sauté the onions in the oil in a large saucepan over medium heat until softened, about 5 minutes. • Add the tomatoes and bell peppers. Cover and simmer over low heat until the sauce has thickened, about 30 minutes. • Stir in the vinegar and cook for 5 minutes. • Add the olives and season with salt. Simmer for 5 minutes. • Garnish with the parsley and serve warm.

6	onions, thinly sliced
1/3	cup (90 ml) extra-virgin olive oil
2	(14-ounce/400-g) cans tomatoes, with juice
2	red bell peppers (capsicums), seeded, cored, and cut into thin slices
2	yellow bell peppers, (capsicums) seeded, cored, and cut into thin slices
2	green bell peppers, (capsicums) seeded, cored, and cut into thin slices
1/3	cup (90 ml) white wine vinegar
1	cup (100 g) pitted green olives, coarsely chopped
	Salt
	Fresh parsley leaves, to garnish

Serves: 6–8
Preparation: 5 minutes
Cooking: 45 minutes
Level: 1

GRILLED SUMMER VEGETABLES

Heat a grill pan over high heat. • Grill the zucchini until tender, 3–5 minutes each side. Set aside. • Grill the bell peppers until tender, 3–5 minutes each side. Set aside. • Brush the eggplant slices lightly with 2 tablespoons of the oil. Place in the grill pan and grill until tender, about 5 minutes each side. • Arrange all the grilled vegetables on a large serving plate. • Season with salt and pepper. Drizzle with the oil and serve hot or at room temperature.

4 medium zucchini (courgettes), thinly sliced lengthwise

1 red bell pepper (capsicum), seeded, cored, and cut into thin slices

1 yellow bell pepper (capsicum), seeded, cored, and cut into thin slices

1 large eggplant (aubergine), thinly sliced

Salt and freshly ground black pepper

1/2 cup (125 ml) extra-virgin olive oil

Serves: 4
Preparation: 15 minutes
Cooking: 30 minutes
Level: 1

GREEK SALAD

Mix the cucumbers, tomatoes, onions, feta, and olives in a salad bowl. • Beat the oil and vinegar in a small bowl until well blended. • Drizzle the dressing over the salad and season with salt and pepper. Toss gently and garnish with the oregano. • Serve at once.

2 cucumbers, thinly sliced

4 firm-ripe tomatoes, coarsely chopped

2 red onions, thickly sliced

4 ounces (125 g) feta cheese, crumbled

1/2 cup (50 g) kalamata olives

5 tablespoons extra-virgin olive oil

2 tablespoons malt or balsamic vinegar

Salt and freshly ground black pepper

Fresh oregano leaves, to garnish

Serves: 2–4
Preparation: 10 minutes
Level: 1

■ ■ ■ *Some people have difficulty digesting cucumbers. If you peel them, they will find them easier to digest.*

NIÇOISE SALAD

Salad: Put the tomatoes in a colander and sprinkle with salt. Let drain for 1 hour. • Arrange the salad greens in individual serving dishes. • Top with the tomatoes, bell pepper, tuna, celery, and shallots in the center. • Wrap the olives up in the anchovy fillets and arrange on top. Add the wedges of egg.

Dressing: Whisk the oil and vinegar in a small bowl until well combined. Season with salt and pepper. • Drizzle the dressing over the salad. • Serve at once.

■ ■ ■ *There are many variations on this classic French salad. Feel free to experiment, but always keep the basic mix of tomato, tuna, eggs, and anchovies.*

Salad

10	medium firm-ripe tomatoes, cut into eight wedges
	Coarse sea salt
2	cups (100 g) mixed salad greens
1	red bell pepper (capsicum), seeded, cored, and cut into thin strips
1³/4	cups (200 g) canned tuna in oil, drained
3	stalks celery, finely chopped
3	shallots, finely chopped
8	black olives
8	anchovy fillets in oil
2	hard-boiled eggs, cut into four wedges

Dressing

1/2	cup (125 ml) extra-virgin olive oil
2	tablespoons white wine vinegar
	Salt and freshly ground black pepper

Serves: 4–6
Preparation: 15 minutes
  + 1 hour to drain
Level: 1

CAPRESE

Cut the tomatoes into slices and arrange on a flat serving dish. • Cut the mozzarella into slices of the same width and alternate with the tomato. • Sprinkle with the basil and drizzle with the oil. Season with salt and pepper. • Serve at once.

8	large firm-ripe salad tomatoes
1	pound (500 g) mozzarella cheese
20	large basil leaves
1/3	cup (90 ml) extra-virgin olive oil
	Salt and freshly ground black pepper

Serves: 4–6
Preparation: 10 minutes
Level: 1

FARRO SALAD

Cook the farro in a large pot of salted, boiling water until tender but still chewy, about 30 minutes. • Drain well and let cool under cold running water. • Drain well and transfer to a large salad bowl. • Add the tomatoes, mozzarella, scallions, basil, capers, and zucchini. Drizzle with the oil and season with salt and pepper. Toss well. • Let stand for 10 minutes before serving.

■ ■ ■ *Farro is an ancient strain of wheat. It contains less gluten than modern strains, so is easier to digest. You may substitute with spelt or pearl barley, if preferred.*

2	cups (400 g) farro
16	cherry tomatoes, cut in half
8	ounces (250 g) mozzarella cheese, diced
6	scallions (spring onions), thinly sliced
15	fresh basil leaves, torn
1/3	cup (60 g) capers preserved in brine, drained
4	small zucchini (courgettes), diced
1/3	cup (90 ml) extra-virgin olive oil
	Salt and freshly ground black pepper

Serves: 6–8
Preparation: 10 minutes + 10 minutes to stand
Cooking: 30 minutes
Level: 1

DESSERTS

APRICOT RISOTTO

Combine the milk, sugar, and vanilla pod in a large saucepan and cook over medium heat until it begins to simmer. Cover and decrease the heat to very low. Do not let the milk boil. • Melt the butter in a large frying pan over low heat. • Add the apricots. Cook, stirring, for 2 minutes. • Stir in the rice and cook over medium heat for 3 minutes, stirring constantly. • Stir in the apple juice and when this has been absorbed, begin stirring in the hot milk, $1/2$ cup (125 ml) at a time. Remove the vanilla pod beforea dding the milk. Cook and stir until each addition has been absorbed and the rice is tender, 15–18 minutes. • Stir the apricot purée into the rice. Spoon into individual serving dishes and sprinkle with the almonds. • Serve hot.

$2^1/2$ **cups (625 ml) milk**

1 **tablespoon sugar**

1 **vanilla pod, or** $1/2$ **teaspoon vanilla extract (essence)**

2 **teaspoons butter**

$1/2$ **cup (90 g) diced dried apricots**

1 **cup (200 g) Italian risotto rice**

1 **cup (250 ml) sparkling apple juice or cider**

$1/3$ **cup (90 ml) apricot purée**

2 **tablespoons slivered almonds, toasted**

Serves: 4
Preparation: 10 minutes
Cooking: 30 minutes
Level: 2

■ ■ ■ *You can prepare apricot purée quickly by mashing 3 or 4 canned apricot halves in a small bowl with a fork.*

BAKLAVA

Baklava: Preheat the oven to 475°F (250°C/gas 9) • Mix the almonds, sugar, and cinnamon in a small bowl. • Brush a 10-inch (25-cm) square pan with the butter. • Cut the sheets of phyllo to the size of the baking pan. • Brush a sheet of phyllo with butter and place in the prepared pan. Brush with more butter. Repeat with two more sheets of phyllo. Sprinkle with the nut mixture. Continue layering the remaining sheets of phyllo and nuts until all the ingredients are used, making sure the top sheet is well buttered. • Cut the top layers of pastry lengthwise into parallel strips. Then cut into diamond shapes about 2 inches (5 cm) in length. Cut through all the layers to the bottom of the pan. • Bake for 30 minutes. • Lower the oven to 300°F (150°C/gas 2) and bake for 1 hour.

Syrup: Bring the superfine sugar, water, cinnamon, orange zest, and honey to a boil in a small saucepan. Simmer for 15 minutes. • Pour the hot syrup over the baklava. Let cool.

Baklava

2 cups (200 g) finely ground almonds

1 cup (200 g) superfine (caster) sugar

1¹/2 teaspoons ground cinnamon

16 sheets phyllo pastry, thawed if frozen

1 cup (250 g) butter, melted

Syrup

3 cups (600 g) superfine (caster) sugar

1¹/2 cups (375 ml) water

1 cinnamon stick

1 piece orange or lemon zest

1 tablespoon honey

Serves: 8–10
Preparation: 35 minutes
Cooking: 1 hour
   30 minutes
Level: 3

RICOTTA CHEESECAKE

Shortcrust Pastry: Combine the flour and salt in a large bowl. • Rub in the butter until the mixture resembles bread crumbs. • Stir in the sugar. • Mix in the egg and enough water to make a firm dough. Knead quickly until smooth. Wrap in plastic wrap (cling film) and chill for 1 hour. • Roll out the pastry on a floured surface to line a 10-inch (25-cm) pie pan. Trim the edges and prick all over with a fork. Chill for 15 minutes. • Preheat the oven to 375°F (190°C/gas 5). • Line the pastry shell with parchment paper and fill with pie weights or dried beans. • Bake for 15 minutes. • Remove the paper and beans. Bake until the pastry is golden, about 5 minutes. • Lower the oven to 350°F (180°C/gas 4).

Ricotta Filling: Beat the ricotta, 1 whole egg and 4 egg yolks, flour, sugar, mixed peel, lemon zest, rum, and cinnamon in a large bowl. • Beat the egg whites until stiff and fold them into the mixture. Spoon the filling into the pastry shell. • Bake until the filling is set, about 1 hour. • Serve warm or chilled.

Shortcrust Pastry

- $1^2/3$ cups (250 g) all-purpose (plain) flour
- Pinch of salt
- $1/2$ cup (125 g) butter, cut up
- 1 tablespoon sugar
- 1 large egg
- 3 tablespoons ice water

Ricotta Filling

- 2 cups (500 g) fresh ricotta cheese
- 1 large egg, lightly beaten, + 4 large eggs, separated
- 3 tablespoons all-purpose (plain) flour
- $1/2$ cup (100 g) sugar
- $1/2$ cup (50 g) diced mixed peel
- 3 teaspoons finely grated lemon zest
- 2 tablespoons rum
- Pinch of ground cinnamon

Serves: 6–8
Preparation: 20 minutes + 75 minutes to chill
Cooking: 1 hour 20 minutes
Level: 3

BANANA BEIGNETS

Combine the flour, confectioners' sugar, baking powder, and salt in a large bowl. • Beat the milk and egg in a small bowl and add to the dry ingredients. • Use a large rubber spatula to fold in the mashed bananas. Add more milk if the mixture is too thick and more flour if too thin. The batter should have a thick dropping consistency. • Heat the oil in a deep-fryer or deep frying pan to very hot. • Drop tablespoons of the batter into the oil. Fry in small batches until golden brown, 5–7 minutes. • Drain on paper towels. Dust with the confectioners' sugar and serve hot.

1^1/$_2$ **cups (225 g) all-purpose (plain) flour**

2 **tablespoons confectioners' (icing) sugar + extra, to dust**

2 **teaspoons baking powder**

^{1}/$_4$ **teaspoon salt**

^{2}/$_3$ **cup (150 ml) milk**

1 **large egg**

3 **bananas, mashed and drizzled with freshly squeezed lemon juice**

4 **cups (1 liter) vegetable oil, to deep-fry**

Serves: 6
Preparation: 5 minutes
Cooking: 20 minutes
Level: 2

■ ■ ■ *These delicious beignets are of French origin. In the United States beignets are one of the most popular foods in New Orleans.*

CATALONIAN CREAM

Dissolve the cornstarch in $1/2$ cup (125 ml) of milk in a small bowl. Set aside. • Bring the remaining $31/2$ cups (825 ml) milk, lemon zest, and cinnamon to a boil in a large saucepan over medium heat. • Beat the egg yolks and sugar in a double boiler with an electric mixer at high speed until pale and thick. • Pour the milk into the egg mixture. Place over barely simmering water and gradually add the cornstarch mixture, stirring constantly. • Bring to a boil and cook, stirring, until the mixture lightly coats a metal spoon or registers 160°F (70°C) on an instant-read thermometer. • Pour into individual ramekins. • Chill for 2 hours before serving.

$1/3$ cup (50 g) cornstarch (cornflour)

4 cups (1 liter) milk

Finely grated zest of 1 lemon

1 teaspoon ground cinnamon

9 large egg yolks

$11/4$ cups (250 g) sugar

Serves: 8
Preparation: 30 minutes + 2 hours to chill
Cooking: 10 minutes
Level: 2

For a delicious caramel topping, mix $1/2$ cup (100 g) of sugar with 3 tablespoons of cold water and cook over low heat until caramelized. Drizzle the caramel over the chilled custards just before serving.

TIRAMISÙ

Beat the egg yolks and sugar in a large bowl with an electric mixer at high speed until pale and thick. • In a separate bowl, beat the egg whites and salt in a medium bowl until stiff peaks form. • Stir the mascarpone into the egg yolk mixture. • Use a large rubber spatula to fold in the beaten whites. • Set out a large square dish. • Spoon one-third of the mascarpone mixture into the dish and sprinkle with half the chocolate. Add a layer of the ladyfingers, dipping them in the coffee before arranging them in the dish. Add another layer of mascarpone cream. Sprinkle with the remaining chocolate and top with the remaining coffee-soaked ladyfingers. Cover with the remaining mascarpone cream. Dust with the cocoa. • Chill for at least 4 hours before serving.

3 large eggs, separated, + 2 large egg yolks

3/4 cup (150 g) sugar

Pinch of salt

2 cups (500 g) mascarpone cheese

8 ounces (250 g) ladyfingers (sponge fingers)

1/2 cup (125 ml) very strong black coffee

5 ounces (150 g) dark chocolate, coarsely grated

2 tablespoons unsweetened cocoa powder

Serves: 6
Preparation: 20 minutes
   + 4 hours to chill
Level: 2

PANNA COTTA WITH RASPBERRY COULIS

Panna Cotta: Set out six $3/4$-cup (180-ml) ramekins. • Soften the gelatin in $1/4$ cup (60 ml) of water in a small bowl. • Bring the milk, cream, and sugar to a boil in a medium saucepan over low heat. • Remove from the heat and stir in the gelatin and almond liqueur until the gelatin has dissolved completely. • Pour the mixture evenly into the ramekins and chill for 4 hours.

Raspberry Coulis: Combine the sugar and water in a small saucepan and simmer over low heat until the sugar has dissolved. • Add the cinnamon, raspberries, and red wine and bring to a gentle boil. Lower the heat and simmer for 5 minutes. • Remove from the heat and discard the cinnamon stick. Strain through a fine-mesh sieve to remove the raspberry seeds. Let cool completely and chill until ready to serve. • Stand the ramekins in boiling water for 1 minute. Turn out onto serving dishes. • Spoon the raspberry coulis over the top and serve.

Panna Cotta

1	tablespoon plain powdered gelatin
$1/4$	cup (60 ml) water
$1^1/2$	cups (375 ml) milk
$1^1/2$	cups (375 ml) heavy (double) cream
$1/2$	cup (100 g) sugar
2	tablespoons almond liqueur

Raspberry Coulis

1	cup (200 g) sugar
$3/4$	cup (180 ml) water
1	cinnamon stick
2	cups (300 g) fresh raspberries
$1/2$	cup (125 ml) good-quality dry red wine

Serves: 6
Preparation: 25 minutes
  + 4 hours to chill
Cooking: 25 minutes
Level: 2

LEMON SORBET

Bring the sugar and water to a boil in a small saucepan. Simmer for 5 minutes, then set aside to cool. • Stir in the lemon juice when the mixture is completely cool. • Beat the egg whites and salt in a large freezerproof bowl with an electric mixer at high speed until stiff peaks form. • Gradually stir in the lemon syrup and place in the freezer. Stir every 30 minutes to make sure it freezes evenly. After 3 hours whisk the mixture, then return to the freezer for 30 minutes more. • Serve in glasses with the strawberries and cookies.

1   cup (200 g) sugar

1^1/$_4$ cups (300 ml) water

Freshly squeezed juice of 4 lemons

3   large egg whites

^{1}/$_8$ teaspoon salt

Sliced strawberries, to serve

Cookies, to serve

Serves: 6
Preparation: 20 minutes
    + 3 hours 30 minutes
    to chill
Cooking: 5 minutes
Level: 1

INDEX